Accountability

It all depends on what you mean

Theo Brooks

Akkad Press

Published by **Akkad Press**, P. O. Box 3076, Clifton, NJ 07012

© 1995 Theo Brooks

All rights reserved. No parts of this book may be reproduced in any form by any electronic or mechanical means (including photocopying, recording or information storage and retrieval) without permission in writing from the author except for brief quotations in review.

Brooks, Theo

Accountability: It all depends on what you mean

Includes illustrations, notes, bibliography, and index

Management and Business
Organizations
Political and Social Issues
Accountability and Responsibility

ISBN 9645322-5-5 (hardback)

ISBN 9645322-6-3 (paperback)

Library of Congress Catalog Card Number 95-94066

Printed in the United States of America

Jacket Design by Edward Smith Design Inc.

Contents

Introduction — 1

Part One

1. Defining Accountability — 7
2. The Accountability Mechanism — 15
3. Accountable for What? — 29
4. Who? To? How? When? What if? — 39
5. Responsibility — 45
6. Direct and Visible Accountability — 49
7. More Types of Accountability — 55
8. The *Challenger* Accident — 65

Part Two

9. Legitimacy — 77
10. Trust — 89
11. Motives and Contracts — 97
12. Only Human — 109
13. Elusive Accountability — 121
14. Hold the Accountability — 129
15. Summary — 137

Part Three

List 1	The Six Accountability Criteria	143
List 2	Accountability Flows	144
List 3	Accountability Pairs	145
List 4	Accountability Diagnostic	146
List 5	Accountability Resources	147
List 6	Accountability Values Inventory	148
List 7	Accountability Values Questionnaire	149
List 8	What Are We Paying for?	151
List 9	Accountability Sound Bites	153
List 10	Legitimacy Sources	154
List 11	Causes of Uncertainty	155
List 12	Variations on Should/Can/Do	156
List 13	Doing right	157
List 14	Unethical Behavior	158

Notes	159
Bibliography	163
Index	165

Acknowledgments

The commitment, encouragement, patience, and enthusiasm of my wife, Grace Roberts, saw this project through. Her actions have given the word "support" more meanings for me than I could possibly enumerate.

My thanks to Paul Edwards both for perspicaciously prodding the argument in its infancy and for a decade and a half of mental challenge.

I am grateful to Andy Beattie, Perian Carson, Joan Beth Lund and Linda Sue Park who read, and offered valuable comments on, the entire manuscript, as the book was nearing completion. My thanks, too, to Paula Martin and Dennis O'Boyle for reading (and enduring) early versions of the argument.

I would like to thank the following for their comments on the manuscript or parts of it: Trevor Day, Neal Grove, Barbara Miller, Nell Minow, Mercedes Rodriguez, and Grant Wiggins. My thanks also to Ray Katz for his encouragement and computer advice.

Many people shared their thoughts on accountability with me in all manner of meetings and surroundings. My thanks to you all.

Naturally, I am responsible for the content. As to whether I am accountable.... well, you'd better read the book!

Please Note

With the exception of a few people and a couple of historical events, e.g., President Roosevelt, the space shuttle *Challenger*, all characters, organizations, and events in this book are entirely fictitious.

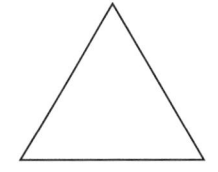

Introduction

This book is a rescue mission to free accountability from the ever-growing army of organizational buzzwords into whose ranks it has been coerced. *Webster's* calls a buzzword an important-sounding word or phrase often of little meaning, adding that it is used chiefly to impress laymen. True. But accountability is not important-sounding: it's important, period. If it has lost its meaning, that is the fault of its users, not the fault of the idea. And accountability should never impress but feel natural and comfortable to everyone.

A mission requires a plan; so the first thing we must do, since buzzwords have a tendency to be vague, is get specific. We must avoid well-worn reactions like throwing our hands up in exasperation and exclaiming: "It's a problem of accountability." That will get us nowhere. To say something is a problem of accountability is rather like me muttering: "There's a problem with the light," if nothing happens when I flick the switch. The problem, when I locate it, is going to be something specific: the bulb, the switch, the wiring, or the power. We need to identify not "a problem of accountability," but specific "accountability problems." To help us, we must ask these questions.

1. What is accountability?

2. How does it work?

3. How can we repair it when it is not working?

4. What right do we have to hold people accountable?

5. When should people be held accountable?

Taken together, these five questions form the vertebrae of the book.

Of accountability's prominence there is no doubt. Nearly everybody has an accountability story: some people have dozens of them. Those who don't have stories chuckle, groan, or flinch involuntarily at the very mention of the word. People seem to view accountability differently. Comments I have heard range from the clear, "It's responsibility," "It's accountancy," "It's motivation," (none of which are true, incidentally), to the mysterious: "I hope everybody's going to buy your book—if only to burn it..." The subtitle, *It all depends on what you mean*, is literally true. You and I may mean something very different when we say "accountability."

How did accountability become this buzzword of many meanings? We cannot know for sure who set accountability on the road to popularity, but by the time of President Nixon's resignation in 1973 the *Christian Science Monitor* was heralding "The Age of Accountability." Nowadays everybody feels free to use it. (I sometimes think, though, that accountants and lawyers believe it belongs to them!) This would be no problem if it were a relatively new word like *aerobics*, *downer*, or *humongous*—all first used in 1967. But accountability has been around for a couple of hundred years, so when its popularity shot up, defining it seemed unnecessary. Everybody assumed everybody else was using the word in the same way.

Managers, politicians, psychologists, educationalists, preachers, everybody began to use it for their own purposes. Accountability turned into a hired gun in organizational warfare. But was it friend or foe? Sometimes accountability did its job properly, but, too often, its effect swung wildly from the lightness of a feather to the force of a 50 megaton nuclear warhead. People were either absurdly *under*accountable or ludicrously *over*accountable.

Let me briefly contrast these important terms. Underaccountability, perhaps the more common of the two complaints, occurs when there is not enough accountability. The type of case that really generates anger is one of incompetence or financial wrongdoing when people talk about accountability, but nothing happens to the senior managers who should be held accountable. To add insult to injury, these managers are later promoted or rewarded in some way.

You can recognize the opposite situation, overaccountability, when the word accountability has become synonymous with finickiness, hassle, a never-ending demand for information, and whimsical decisions. In short: accountability has become oppressive. Too often, people find themselves being forced to devote so much time to giving reports, writing reports, or collecting figures and information for reports that they are never able to do the work that is the subject of the report!

But both views miss the real point. *Accountability is a balance* and I aim to show that we are not doomed to fall on one side of the scale or the other.

I have written this book in the belief that however you define yourself, "manager," "executive," "customer," "voter," "parent," or whatever, accountability can be turned into a real asset. But I have had to narrow my approach in the interest of presenting an argument that is coherent and manageable.

1. I have chosen to emphasize accountability in the workplace. For one thing, I have been advising managers for the majority of my career and I know this area well. For another, having a job is an experience most of us share. The examples, however, are not all work related.

2. I often use the general word "organization" because accountability applies equally to a business, a government department, a nonprofit, a school, a hospital, a science laboratory, a warship, or an art gallery.

3. When I use the term "manager," I am not just referring to people who have the title "manager" but to anyone in any position of authority. Supervisors, CEOs, doctors, politicians, vice presidents, teachers, and board members are all managers. In my scheme of things, customers, voters, and parents are managers too.

I would not have written a book about accountability unless I had thought it was important. Let me conclude these introductory remarks by saying how important I think it is. *Accountability is to organizations what breathing is to bodies.* You may not notice it all the time, but when it is in trouble, everything else is in trouble. If you sense your organization needs to breathe better, check accountability.

Part One

Chapters 1 through 7 answer the questions: "What is accountability?" "How does accountability work?" and "How can we repair accountability if it is not working?" By the end of chapter 7, you will have the means to evaluate the state of accountability in whatever setting is important to you.

In chapter 8, I analyze a well-known event to show the serious consequences of ignoring or misunderstanding accountability. Every reader will remember the loss of the space shuttle *Challenger* and its crew on January 28, 1986. The whole business was an accountability disaster. As you read this chapter, you will realize that the types of accountability errors involved in the *Challenger* tragedy are no different from errors made in other organizations. The only real difference is that the consequences for *Challenger* were so dramatic and tragic. *Challenger* speaks to anyone interested in accountability.

1

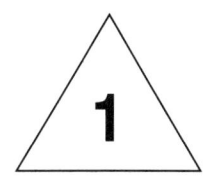

Defining Accountability

As children, we learn the basics of accountability as soon as we learn the relationship between cause and effect. The world becomes our laboratory. We drop something: it breaks. We hit people: they cry out in pain. We quickly discover that cause and effect apply to us too. If we embarrass or anger adults by complaining, attacking our weaker siblings, or stealing from the local store, we are scolded or worse. We are told that our behavior not only does but should have consequences for us; and not any consequences, but ones that "match" our deeds. This is how we are meant to learn our society's views of right and wrong, justice and fairness.

We may provisionally conclude from our early experiments that there is an apparent relationship between how we act and what happens to us; trivial actions lead to trivial consequences, serious actions to serious consequences. If we drew a graph, we might represent our findings like this:

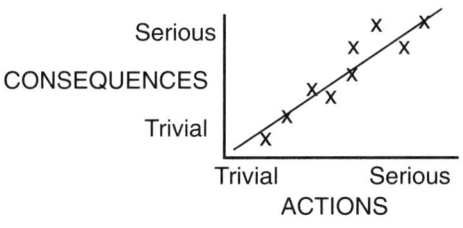

Fig. 1.1: Idealized Graph

Some children are never exposed to this relationship, and even this simple notion of accountability may remain very alien to them. Even if we do learn it, as we get to know the world better, its people, and its organizations, we find that our graph is a poor representation of the relationship. Actions and consequences are not linked naturally in the way that dropping a plate leads to it cracking, or failing to fill up with gas results in the car stopping. We meet poor teachers who waste our time and theirs but are allowed to go on teaching year after year. We learn that adults say one thing and do another. The supposed ideal relationship all too often turns out to be much more random than we supposed, and consequences bear little or no relationship to actions. Serious actions can have trivial consequences and trivial actions, serious consequences. We mentally tear up our graph and draw another:

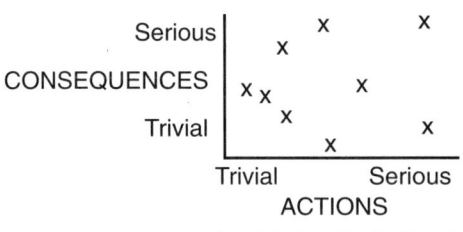

Fig. 1.2: Real Life Graph

Yet the imprint of the first graph never disappears completely, and, for many of us, it remains the most influential benchmark against which we measure our actions. But if our daily experience mocks the proposition that consequences should match actions, how are we to hold on to the idea of right and wrong, of justice, of fairness? We need to build a correcting mechanism which we call accountability.

Neutral and Strong Accountability

Anyone who wants to build an accountability mechanism has to make a choice between two competing uses of the word accountability which I call *neutral* and *strong*. The neutral use means, literally, having to give an account, an explanation, or a justification. The strong use demands not only that an account be given but that *the person being held accountable should incur sanctions if the account is unsatisfactory*. In other words, "having to give an account," by itself, is insufficient.

To be serious about accountability, we must adopt the strong use because the recurring lack of sanctions is one of the main reasons accountability has become a buzzword. We talk about accountability when it is unclear, in the way we talk about honesty when we meet lies or trust when we feel betrayed. To use strong accountability is to reforge the link between actions and consequences.

For many of us, justifying our actions is sanction enough, especially if personal or professional honor is at stake. Who needs additional sanctions when giving an account produces more than enough guilt and gloom? But to rely on guilt as a sanction is inadequate, even slippery, because what sends Dick into fits of despair may be water off Jane's back.

Getting people to justify or explain themselves, whatever the emotional consequences, does not make them more accountable. For example, say you are my manager, and every Monday I tell you what I did the previous week. I am accountable to you in the neutral sense: I give an account. If you then ask me to explain what I am doing every day instead of every week and request five reports instead of one, those demands do not, in the strong sense, make me any more accountable. They just mean I report more frequently and in greater detail. Suppose I am performing poorly and you are doing nothing about it, then talking to you every day and giving you a whole wad of reports is irrelevant to my accountability. The first question you should ask when you hear the words "accountable" and "accountability" is: What credible sanctions, if any, are involved here? More accounts do not necessarily mean more accountability.

Not Just Numbers

Another common mistake is to assume that, because accountability is obviously related to the word "count," it must always involve numbers. This misapprehension is fueled by accountants, armed with financial statements and quarterly reports, seeking the Grail of Financial Accountability. But numbers in isolation mean nothing. If they are going to serve as evidence of the existence of accountability, they must be judged in context.

For example, high turnover is often interpreted as a symptom of organizational malaise and may reflect badly on a manager who has to explain her management performance. But high turnover is nothing more than a set of numbers. Paint the context. Perhaps high turnover in a particular department is a recent and unusual phenomenon; maybe the manager trains people so well that they soon go on to better things; the industry as a whole could be expanding, drawing people away; or perhaps staff who leave are attracted to organizations with better pay and benefits.

This is not to say that numbers should be ignored. They provide a certain objectivity and are often the principal measure of organizational achievement. But the context of the numbers must be treated with care. Ask yourself whether the figures *really* indicate that the department is improving/going downhill/operating efficiently/fulfilling its expectations, or however you interpret them. Are there alternative interpretations?

The need for interpretation is evidence that accountability is more than counting. If accountability were confined to things we could count easily: the number of dollars in a bank account; the number of beds in a hospital; the average number of minutes to takes to answer a customer inquiry; the additional power drills sold at stores in a given area, following a local advertising campaign, it would be much easier to repair than it is, and it would never have achieved its current prominence.

But we also want to hold people accountable for things that are harder to count, in particular, their general behavior. One option is to reduce the uncountable to something we can count. The danger here is that in order to reduce we have to distort. Take education and training. There is a growing tendency to reduce everything in these fields to "skills." Once skills have been isolated they can be counted individually—skill 1, skill 2, skill 3 etc.—and each skill can be measured (counting again). If counting is all you want to do, and skills are the only thing that can be counted, then, of course, everything is going to look like a skill. But effective managers and educated students are more than the sum of their skills.

Only through very limited activities can we hold others accountable for their individual skills. Mostly, we want to hold them accountable for their integrated behavior. To do this, we have to exercise our judgment. And exercising our judgment, like interpretation, goes beyond counting.

Not Just Laws

The power of accountants to shape our perception of accountability is equaled only by that of lawyers. When reference books fail to speak to accountability, they usually send readers to the law: "see law," "see liability," "see criminal liability." Where else but in courts might you find such a clear-cut link between actions and consequences? Courts are theaters of accountability, but do they match consequences to actions any better than other theaters of human life? The legal system is adversarial and the objective of lawyers is not to match consequences to actions but to win battles for the hearts and minds of the judge, the jury, and the growing television audience. Matching and winning may overlap—friends of justice sincerely hope they do—but overlaps are not guaranteed. Cynics may even say they are coincidental. If your view of the law is becoming a little jaded, it is time to reeducate yourself about the true nature of accountability.

Defining Accountability

Defining accountability can be delayed no longer. The definition that underlies much of what I say in this book is this:

Accountability is a mechanism to ensure that individuals can be called to account for their actions, and that sanctions are incurred if the account is unsatisfactory.

Four words require further comment:

Mechanism. When I use the word mechanism, I have two things in mind: a procedure and an object. If I say that a bill now before Congress will create a mechanism to stop companies from evading taxes, readers will understand I am talking about a procedure. But we can also learn a great deal about accountability if we compare it to a physical mechanism. As with physical mechanisms, good design helps and maintenance is essential. An energy source is required as it is possible to have a well constructed, well maintained mechanism that does not work. A car engine needs gas; a fridge needs electricity; accountability needs commitment (and other things). Someone has to start accountability since it cannot get going by itself. If a mechanism has not deteriorated too much, it can be repaired; otherwise, it needs to be totally replaced. The same applies to accountability.

Individuals. This book is aimed at individuals, which is why I use the word in the definition. Nevertheless, we often treat organizations, groups, or departments as if they were individuals—a reasonable and legal thing to do. It is not unusual to start sentences with "Our company should be accountable for.....," "My department cannot be held accountable for.....," and so on. Expect to meet this collective use as you go through the book.

Sanctions. Sanctions are so important to the subject of this book that I introduced them even before I defined accountability. If I am your manager and we are talking about accountability, then I must make clear to you that *the purpose of sanctions is not to act as a threat to you but as a guarantee to me.* Just as a central heating boiler kicks in when the temperature in the room drops below a certain level, so accountability kicks in when performance or behavior drops below a certain level.

It is rather like using clocks in competitive chess to ensure that games are finished in evenings rather than lifetimes. A common rule is that each player has two and a half hours to play the first forty moves and less time for further moves as the game progresses. The rule is not designed to threaten the players but to guarantee that the action (such as it is in chess) moves along. Certainly, players who have one minute left to make eleven moves may feel pressured, but that is not the purpose of having a time limit. Good players continue to analyze the board even when time is tight. Similarly, the purpose of accountability sanctions is to move the action of an organization along; accountability is indifferent to what the members of the organization think. Does the clock care what the chess players think?

Unsatisfactory. Values in any society, in its organizations, and in its businesses evolve over time. This evolution does not occur with everyone marching in step like cadets on the drill field of a military academy. Values are in a state of constant flux. Does the word "satisfactory" mean the same to you as it does to your colleagues and friends? It is no surprise that there is a wide variety of "cultures" in organizations because organizational values vary so much.

For this reason, an accountability mechanism will always be slightly imprecise. For example, say you, as my manager, offer me this deal: You will be promoted if you complete this project in a timely fashion. We both agree that the action of completing the project is directly related to the consequence of my getting a promotion. I will not get the promotion if I fail or am late. So the overall accountability mechanism is in place. But the seeds of a dispute have been sown because the word "timely" is vague. We may interpret "timely" very differently and argue about it. But whatever our disagreements, they take place *within* the mechanism of accountability.

To explain what I mean by saying the disagreement takes place "within the mechanism," I must show how the mechanism works.

2

The Accountability Mechanism

To understand an unfamiliar mechanism, we must first be able to recognize its components. Accountability has only six, and to identify them we must answer the following questions:

1. Who is giving the account?

2. To whom is the account to be given?

3. For what action or job is the account to be given?

4. How is the account to be given?

5. When is the account to be given?

6. What happens if the account is unsatisfactory?

It doesn't matter what organization you work for or what position you hold, if you claim that accountability exists, you must be able to answer all six questions credibly. If just one component is absent, accountability does not exist. For example, you may be able to give satisfactory answers to all the questions except: When is the account to be given? If we do not know when a mechanism operates, how can we say it is fully operational? This also means that strengthening an individual component only increases accountability if the other components are firmly in place. Changing the oil in the engine of your car will make it run better, but not if the battery is dead. You will become a better analyst of accountability if you start each time from the assumption that not a single component exists.

I have reduced the questions to a simple list, and collectively labeled them the *accountability criteria*.

> *Who?*
>
> *To?*
>
> *For?*
>
> *How?*
>
> *When?*
>
> *What if?*

When somebody asks whether accountability exists in a given situation, the answer must always be: Check the criteria. They lie at the heart of accountability and are so important that if you remember only one thing from this book, remember this list. And why these particular criteria? I think 1, 2, and 3 are self-evident. Without criteria 4 and 5 accountability will exist only on paper. Criterion 6 ensures the existence of sanctions if the account, report, or justification is unsatisfactory.

Here are a couple of straightforward examples that show the criteria at work. A specialist is accountable to a manager for doing an agreed job or set of jobs. The account is given in meetings both formal and informal. In most organizations, specialists can be held accountable at almost any time. Sanctions will vary, but traditionally the ultimate sanction is dismissal. We arrive at the following table:

Who?	Specialist
To?	Manager
For?	Doing an agreed job satisfactorily
How?	Meetings, appraisals
When?	On demand/regularly
What if?	Dismissal

In the next example, the person receiving the account is not a manager within an organization but a customer; and the account is being given not by an individual but by a company. (Note that, although the company is the *Who?* the sale will be conducted by an individual *agent* of the company.) The company is accountable to the customer for delivering a satisfactory product. The *How?* and *When?* of giving the account take place when the customer receives the product and starts to use it. If the product does not work, the customer has two obvious sanctions: go elsewhere, or get refunds or replacements. Again we can construct a simple table:

Who?	Company
To?	Customer
For?	Delivering a satisfactory product
How?	When the customer uses the product
When?	Any time after the sale
What if?	Go elsewhere or get a refund

Units of Accountability

Taken together, the criteria form a *unit of accountability*. Readers who prefer to visualize arguments can put the criteria into triangles and "map" accountability unit by unit. I have called this method *Triangular Mapping*. Look at this "map."

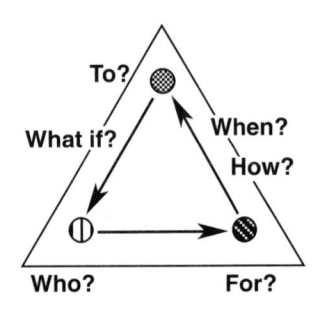

Fig. 2.1: Basic Unit of Accountability

To "read" it, start from the bottom left. In order for the *Who?* to be accountable, accountability must "flow" through the *For?* until it reaches the *To?* Before then, it must pass through the *How?* and the *When?* If these are not firmly in place, the flow dries up. The *To?* is not the final destination. The flow must have the *potential* of returning to the *Who?* via the *What if?* criterion. The boundary around the mechanism reminds us that each unit of accountability must be treated as a whole and separately from other units.

Once you are aware of separate units of accountability, the fundamental way to improve or repair accountability problems immediately becomes clear: *analyze accountability one unit at a time*. You will soon identify any weaknesses. The data of the specialist from the previous section generates the following map:

Fig. 2.2: Specialist's Unit of Accountability

The company's data generates this map:

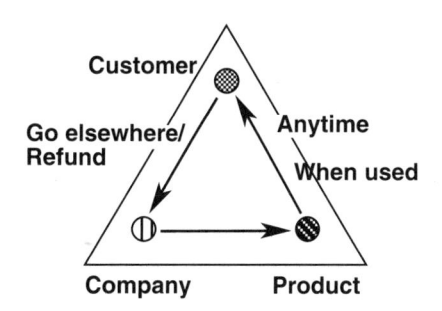

Fig. 2.3: Company's Unit of Accountability

If the flow of accountability has been interrupted or has dried up in part of the unit, we can represent that too. For example, neutral accountability—the absence of sanctions—which I described in the previous chapter, is represented in Fig. 2.4.

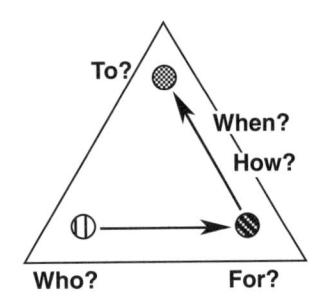

Fig. 2.4: Neutral Accountability

The worst case is when there is absolutely no flow at all, accountability's "absolute zero." All we know is that nobody is accountable to anybody for anything!

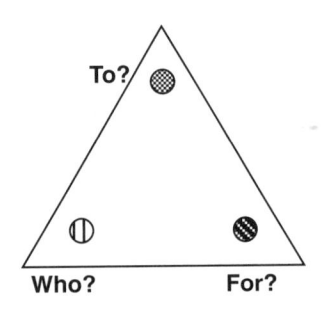

Fig. 2.5: Absolute Zero Accountability

Chains and Charts

Units are separate entities but they are never isolated. They are chained together as in the map opposite (Fig. 2.6). In accountability terms, managers have two roles: *Who?* in one unit and *To?* in the other. (I shall be introducing a third later.) So one way to think about organizations is to imagine them as nothing but chains of units of accountability.

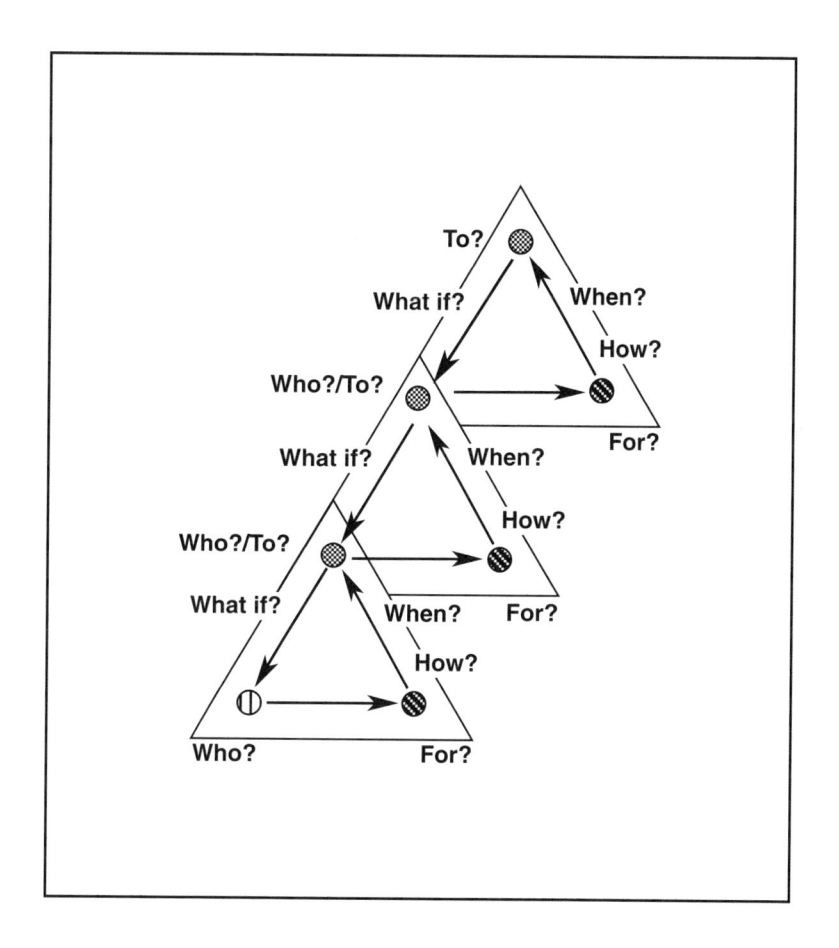

Fig. 2.6: Chain of Accountability

Although a chain of units bears a resemblance to a traditional organization chart, do not presume that accountability is merely another way of describing the structure of an organization. *The accountability mechanism is independent of formal structures* and does not care what it is being applied to, in the same way an electric current does not care whether it is powering a food processor or a factory.

There are two points of difference between an organization chart and a chain of accountability. An organization chart usually answers only two of the six criteria questions, *Who?* and *To?* as you can see on this small representative organization chart.

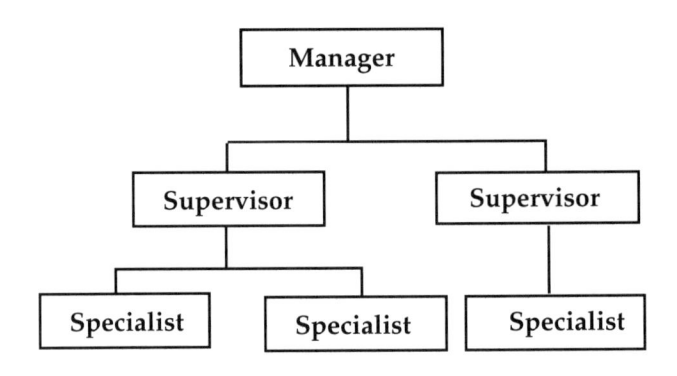

Fig. 2.7: Typical Organization Chart

The other four criteria, *For? How? When?* and *What if?* are subject to considerable uncertainty which I shall describe in the next two chapters. Second, even small organizations have dozens of chains made up of hundreds of units.

In the eyes of accountability, the traditional model of organization structure, the much-attacked hierarchy, is neither good nor bad. It is possible, in principle, for full accountability to exist in a complex hierarchy and to be totally absent in a simple one. "Simpler means better" is not always the case.

Take a company that has ten levels of management with accountability functioning properly at all levels. After a restructuring exercise, only four levels remain. Accountability should be stronger because it has to "flow" through fewer units. But, if the restructuring results in the remaining managers having too much work to do, the accountability mechanism may break down through neglect.

Accountability is like the party game "telephone" or "whispers" where a message is whispered by one person to another. When the message has to go through 20 people it often becomes garbled. Sending the message through only four people should keep it intact. Yet, if those 20 people play with care and commitment, the message will successfully flow through the group to its destination. Conversely, it takes only one person who is dull, careless, or doesn't want to play to sabotage the four-person chain. Attention and commitment lubricate accountability.

Central Servers

As well as being parts of chains, units of accountability compete against each other. To illustrate this I shall restrict the units to two. There could, of course, be many.

I have labeled this common situation the *central server* problem. It occurs when one person is accountable to two or more people. For example, if a single word processing specialist services three or four equal partners who are constantly demanding that their individual work be completed "Yesterday!" accountability will be dissipated unless the central server has a system or protocol for distinguishing among the competitors. A lack of guidance is likely to create tension and undermine the performance of even the best-organized central servers.

Central servers exist at all levels of an organization: project managers caught between the needs of two departments; school principals juggling the demands of the education department and the demands of parents; sales people balancing the requests of two different customers. No one is immune. A CEO is a central server accountable to both shareholders and customers.

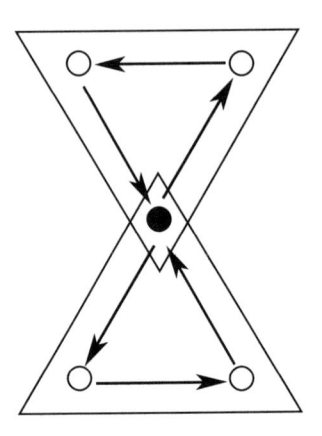

Fig. 2.8: Central Server

Jobs, actions, and tasks can also be caught between units. The most common symptom of this condition is a turf war which is nothing but competition between different units of accountability. In a turf war, the job is a prize worth winning, which is why it is caught in the middle. Because it brings resources, power, or prestige in its wake, people *want* to be accountable for it!

The Manager's Three Roles

I said earlier that a manager has three roles. Let me now state clearly what these roles are.

1. The Manager as *To?*

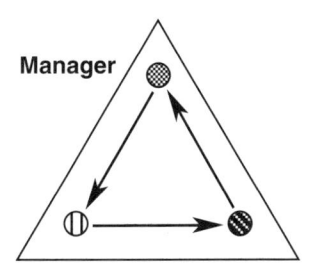

Fig. 2.9: Manager as *To?*

In this type of unit managers *receive* the account—someone is accountable to them. In most cases, of course, they will have to handle many units of this type and do what is necessary to ensure that every unit is performing well.

2. The Manager as *Who?*

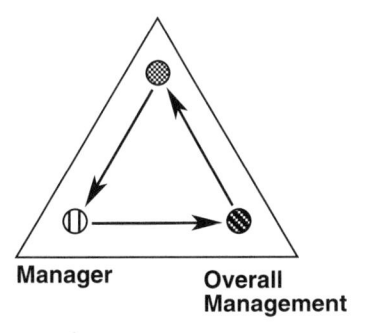

Fig. 2.10: Manager as *Who?*

In this type of unit managers *give* the account and have to explain their management actions. This will include justifying the performance of every unit accountable to them, organizing the work, and dealing with other sections and departments. Some managers are tempted to get too bogged down with this role and pay less attention to the details of the performance of their own staff—the nitty-gritty of every unit in which they are designated the *To?*

3. The Manager's own job.

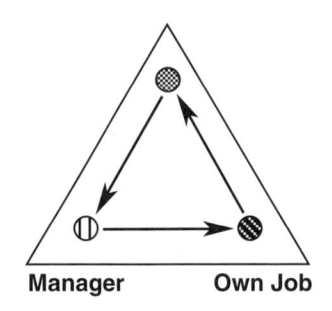

Fig. 2.11: The Manager's Own Job

In addition to the managing role (role 2), many managers have their own particular work for which they are accountable to someone else. We are talking here about jobs that are special to them. When they are under time pressure, or the first two roles simply take up too much time, role 3 often gets completed at nights or on weekends.

Flux and Maintenance

Unfortunately, the accountability mechanism is not as simple as the triangles suggest. It is potentially unstable. The answers to the criteria questions seldom remain constant for very long. People change. Jobs change. People change jobs. Jobs change people. Organizations are in continuous flux and nothing is chiselled in stone. Units are born and die to the rhythm of organizational expansion and contraction.

Like all mechanisms, the accountability mechanism is subject to failure and needs maintenance. Failing to constantly check is the equivalent of never looking under the hood of your car or never backing up your computer files. If you are a manager and a new member of staff joins your department, review the units of accountability throughout your department after, say, a month. The mere presence of a new person may subtly alter the answers to the criteria questions. Suppose Louise joined your department a month ago. If you now ask your staff what her influence has been, you may hear things like this:

"Louise needs time to learn this..." *This could mean*: Do not expect the work to be done quickly.

"I've asked Louise to help me with this..." *This could mean*: Jobs have been split and what individuals should be held accountable for is now unclear.

"Louise doesn't know how things work around here..." *This could mean*: Sanctions may be unclear.

"I assumed you would now get Louise to do this report and free me to do other things..." *This could mean*: The *Who?* in some units of accountability has changed.

Perhaps Louise's impact is only a ripple on the surface of organizational flux. The following may cause waves or even a tsunami or two: the department is understaffed; staff are absent, sick, golfing, out to lunch, on the phone to a friend, or getting a coffee; staff are working slowly; staff are highly energized; posts remain unfilled and everyone is getting behind; half a dozen terrific candidates are interviewed for one vacancy; a piece of unrepaired equipment causes a major slowdown; a supervisor is making poor decisions. And so the ocean of organizational flux heaves away day after day, hour after hour, minute after minute. But if you believe that a small event can have huge consequences you also realize that flux makes prediction hard.

Readers who have not given much thought to flux may get depressed by all this uncertainty, but we really can hold people accountable! I am simply trying to paint the context in which the accountability mechanism operates. We naturally attempt to impose order on the uncertainty that surrounds us, and if we did not assume a certain amount of stability, we would never plan or get anything accomplished. For very good reasons we ignore flux, but it is liable to surprise us when we forget it entirely. When people are part of a mechanism, do not expect them to behave mechanistically. An organization chart gives an illusory impression of stability and order. A major strength of the accountability mechanism, as you will start to see in the next few chapters, is that it can impose order while simultaneously accommodating flux.

3

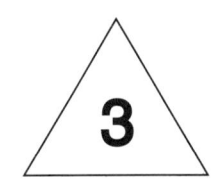

Accountable for What?

All the accountability criteria must be present for accountability to exist, but not all of them are of equal weight. From the definition of accountability, you will have gathered that the *What if?* criterion—What happens if the account is unsatisfactory?—is, perhaps, the most important because it is involved in the first key choice to be made, the one between strong and neutral accountability. But the *For?* criterion—For what action is the account to be given?—runs it a close second. The ramifications of this criterion are so wide-ranging that I am devoting a whole chapter to them. In the following chapter, I shall discuss the other criteria.

Accountability Boundaries

At first glance, any job, action, task, deed, or project that we hold someone accountable for seems to be a simple issue of defining boundaries. If I am Dennis's manager and I ask myself what I am holding him accountable for, the answer will be: Dennis is accountable for x, y, and z.

But this is only half the question. A boundary defines not only what is included but what is excluded. Though San Diego and Tijuana are next door to each other, the U.S.-Mexico border defines San Diego as included in United States and Tijuana as excluded.

If Dennis and I work in the finance department of a company, he knows that, unless I tell him otherwise, public relations will be excluded from his field of accountability. But even this is not straightforward. Although Dennis may respect the creative and literary talents of our colleagues in public relations, he may want to have a say in how much money they spend; hence a potential competition—a turf war—between our unit and theirs, with "allocating money" in the middle. Notice I say "our unit." I'm Dennis's manager. I'm involved too.

To reframe the question in terms of what is being excluded, we must ask: What am I *not* holding this person accountable for? This is particularly useful for a manager who is doing nearly the same job as the person he is managing, or who has to manage jobs so vaguely defined that important work is falling through the cracks.

If we combine the two questions, the accountability boundary question becomes: What are definitely my decisions and jobs, and what are definitely those of people who report to me? A manager who fails to ask this double-barreled question may be expecting too much or too little. Too much, and the accountable person is overaccountable and cannot get the job (or jobs) done. Too little, and he is underaccountable and boredom sets in, wasting the organization's time and money. Worse, the manager may even be doing the work that another person—probably someone who reports to him—is paid to do!

If you are unsure of someone's accountability boundaries, a good approach is to move from the known to the unknown. First, you need to determine what you are absolutely sure the person is accountable for. Once you have established this, you can adopt an approach in which you examine hypothetical situations and gradually push out the boundaries: Accountable for *a*? Yes. For *b*? Maybe. For *c*? No, and so on. Or you might try a reverse approach by asking: What is this person not accountable for? Definitely not *c*. What if *b* were the case? Maybe. And so on, moving backwards.

Style

Related to boundaries is the issue of *style*. In practice, *what* people do cannot easily be separated from *how* they do it. Style is tied up with content and, therefore, if we draw accountability boundaries and hold people accountable for content, it looks as though we must hold them accountable for style as well. Two employees, Graham and Jim, have identical jobs and both achieve similar results. But Jim volunteers to carry out tasks that are not part of his job. He is enthusiastic, cooperative, and follows procedures even when they inconvenience him. If Graham's results are satisfactory, are we going to hold him accountable for being less cooperative and less enthusiastic than Jim?

This is the dilemma. On the one hand, if we hold people accountable for how they do things as well as what they do, we may be holding them accountable for personality traits. Is this right or realistic? Perhaps it is better to leave personality out of the picture altogether. And not just personality. If an employee refuses to work late because she has to pick up her child from day care at a certain time, should we hold her accountable for demonstrating insufficient enthusiasm? On the other hand, if job style is linked to job content, why should it be left out of the accountability reckoning? The job is the whole job, content and style.

The more specifically we can define units of accountability, the better they will work, so our first concern should be to get the content clear. (For example, see List 8 on page 151.) It would, however, be literally inhuman not to be influenced by style. Who is not going to be cheered up by someone doing that little bit extra? An honest message a manager can give staff is this: My aim is to hold you accountable for what you do. I may not be able to hold you accountable for the way you do it—your style—but I am bound to be influenced by it.

Accountability Resources

A well-known Bible story tells how Moses leads the Israelites out of bondage in the land of Egypt. Pharaoh, the Egyptian king, takes some persuading. When he is first approached, not only does he not heed the command: "Let my people go," he actually forces the Israelites to work harder by not giving them straw to make bricks. They now have to scout around the countryside to try and find stubble instead of straw, and they still have to make the same number of bricks! Managers who do not provide the resources needed to do a job are Pharaohs forcing their staff to make bricks without straw.

If the accountability mechanism is to work properly, people need these resources:

1. Authority   to get the job done.

2. Autonomy   so they can get on with the job.

3. Support   especially time, money, and equipment.

4. Information sufficient and relevant.

It is especially easy to neglect sufficient authority. When you are planning a new task, always ensure that those who have to carry it out have enough authority because in each job there is a symmetry between accountability and authority. Projects can be held back if the person who is ultimately accountable is not given the clout to get things done.

Managers must also appreciate that there are times when staff need autonomy and should be left alone. This is not the same as blind trust. It is possible to delegate and still keep an eye on what is happening.

Time, money, and equipment are always a source of tension because, even if the task is clearly defined, you can never be sure how many resources are "enough."

The inclusion of information in the inventory should surprise no one since we live in an information age. Surrounded as we are by phrases like "information society," "information highway," and "information technology," the problem is often too much information. Computers have seen to that, but they can hardly be blamed. If managers plan to hold people accountable, they have to relay the right information. But even though there is more information going around, its possession remains a source of power, and there is considerable temptation to hoard it.

I pointed out earlier that accountability is not usually just about numbers, and even when it is, numbers have to be placed in context. Similarly, resources may appear sufficient, but the specialist or manager must possess sufficient will to use them. Put another way: the means to carry out a task cannot easily be separated from the strength of will that the task requires. This difficulty is compounded because will, unlike most resources, can't be counted. We all know managers who succeed when resources are few by providing their own resources of will and ingenuity. No wonder we call them resourceful!

Accountability Values

I call the final element of the *For?* criterion accountability values, and they are best approached through a questionnaire. Suppose I am a sales manager and you, my boss, are going to hold me accountable for increasing sales by 15% in the next two quarters. The numbers are clear; the time frame is clear. Although rather stretched, I probably have enough resources. As our meeting draws a close, I ask you the following questions. To make them harder, but the points clearer, imagine you are allowed to answer only Yes or No. What would you answer?

1. Is the means I use to achieve the target important, or should I cut corners to meet it at all costs? For example, do you want my staff to skip briefings on a new product that is vital for the company in the long-term? In the short-term these briefings will seriously cut into the time available to make our goal.

2. If I meet the target with some fancy financial juggling, I may look efficient, but in the long-term that may not be very effective. Does it matter?

3. If I devise and you approve a good plan that is derailed by a natural disaster, a shortage of raw materials, or a strike, will these impediments be taken into consideration when my work is evaluated?

4. If my staff and I are clearly working as hard as we can, are we only to be evaluated by our success, or, if we fall a little short, will our effort be taken into account when the project is evaluated?

5. If I have the power to order more stock from our manufacturing department on a hunch that demand for our products will increase beyond our current projections, is it worth taking the risk? Or shall we play safe and wait for the orders to come in?

6. Is a 14.6% rather than a 15% increase in sales good enough, especially if we get good quality sales with likely repeat orders beyond the next two quarters?

7. In order to bump up sales, should we, based on highly selective data, make claims for our products that may not be illegal but may mislead potential buyers?

8. If something unforeseeable goes wrong with one of our products, am I going to be held accountable?

There are no right or wrong answers here, and different people will give different replies. The point is that, however specifically you define a job or task and however carefully you prepare the resources, your values will, in large part, determine your decisions.

In the questionnaire, I highlighted eight of the most common dilemmas:

end results (ends)	or	means to the end (means)
effectiveness	or	efficiency
good results	or	good decisions
successes	or	attempts at success
taking risks	or	playing it safe
quantity	or	quality
doing right	or	avoiding wrong
consequences	or	only the actions

I guarantee, manager or no, you have been confronted by some, perhaps all, of these choices. They are the reason that the seemingly rational approach to management, set objectives and get people to meet them—"management by objectives"—often fails. Objectives are walls held together by the seldom noticed mortar of values. When put under severe pressure, even the strongest mortar crumbles, and with it the wall.

But this is an opportunity! It is very difficult to talk about values in the workplace. They are frequently, and mistakenly, considered a personal issue. An organization with few commonly agreed standards of behavior is inviting trouble. My approach to accountability, with its triangular maps and its demand that the meaning of the criteria be spelled out, gives you an opportunity to bring a little objectivity to any discussion of ethical behavior.

One more analogy. Imagine that a job someone is being held accountable for is represented as a ball sitting on a solid empty table (Fig. 3.1). At first glance, it seems that describing the position of the ball, i.e. defining the job, will be easy. But it isn't. In reality, the ball is bobbing round in a pool, being pushed hither and thither by the currents and eddies of accountability values (Fig. 3.2). If that isn't enough, everyone has a different view of the pool! Don't ignore the currents: chart them.

Further discussion:

To see how values play out in your own organization, see list 7 on page 149. For ideas on distinguishing between avoiding wrong and doing right, see list 13 on page 157.

A Note on Empowerment

Like accountability, "empowerment" has become a buzzword, although one much harder to rescue. It is closely related to the *For?* of accountability and to boundaries and resources in particular. In a way, empowerment is nothing more than redefining accountability boundaries, plus, if the empowered person is lucky, increasing the accountability resources—

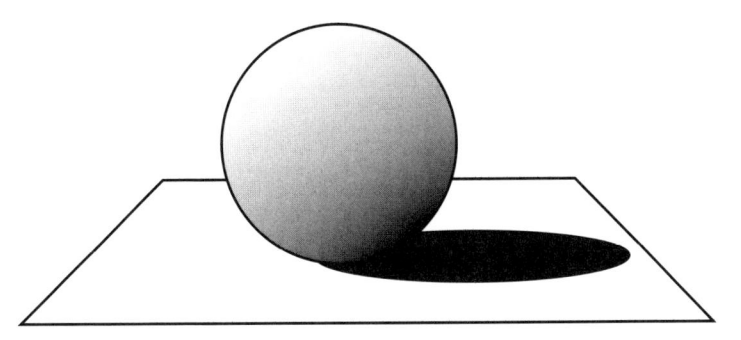

Fig. 3.1: Accountability as a Ball

Fig. 3.2: Accountability Pushed in All Directions

authority, in particular. Redefining boundaries usually means being accountable for more, and many people will not actively seek more authority, unless their organization has put its accountability house in order.

4

Who? To? How? When? What if?

I hope the previous chapter left you in no doubt that checking the criteria needs care. But now the point has been made, five more chapters like that, one for each criterion, and you might begin to wilt! But if we maintain our questioning attitude, it is unnecessary to tackle the rest in such detail. In this chapter, I shall introduce all five remaining criteria, *Who? To? How? When?* and *What if?* with the aim of highlighting some of the problems they may generate.

Who?

Even this innocuous criterion is not entirely straightforward. Suppose something has happened, and we are trying to decide whether to hold Herb accountable. Three situations may lead us astray:

1. We have made a mistake and Herb is simply the *wrong person* because he had nothing to do with what happened.

2. Herb made a mistake and appears to be the person we should hold accountable, but Rick, who delegated this job to Herb, should have done it himself. We are examining the *wrong unit* of accountability. Rick rather than Herb should be the *Who?*

3. What happened is something that *no one should be held accountable for* in the first place. What Herb did happened during his lunch break. Is that any of our concern? Probably not. (But if he is doing drugs, should we try and stop him, or only intervene when his job performance is affected?)

Taken together, we can call these situations *misdirected accountability* and we can represent them in Triangular Mapping terms like this:

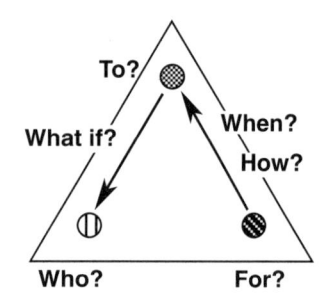

Fig. 4.1: Misdirected Accountability

A person has to give an account and may be subject to sanctions, but the link between the *Who?* and the *For?* is unclear.

To?

We have already identified the major difficulty with this criterion, a central server who is accountable to two or more people. Here are two more problems.

Split Group. You may find yourself, especially if you are a senior executive, accountable to a group of people like a board of directors. The group to whom you are accountable may be divided on an issue or more interested in their own battles than in your accountability to them. Unfortunately, you remain accountable to the whole group when things go wrong.

Bypassed Supervisor. The bypassed supervisor is a common problem. I have used "supervisor" to distinguish between the units of accountability, but this could apply at any level in an organization. Here, the accountability mechanism exists on paper, but, in practice, the manager bypasses the supervisor and goes straight to the specialist. The supervisor-specialist unit of accountability is defunct, but the manager-supervisor unit is still operational. The manager is sabotaging the supervisor, though the supervisor is still fully accountable to the manager. The specialist is now a central server who has to choose between the manager and the supervisor:

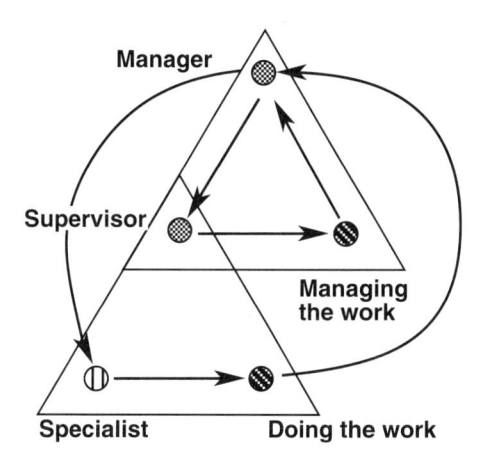

Fig. 4.2 The Bypassed Supervisor

What should you do if something comparable to the bypassed supervisor happens in your department?

1. If the manager and specialist are friends or longtime colleagues, the position of the supervisor needs to be respected.

2. If the supervisor cannot do the job, the manager must take action: support, train, or transfer the supervisor.

3. If the manager is a compulsive meddler, the obvious answer is that he should just stop it, although, for many, this advice will be impossible to take!

4. If a specialist who reports to a supervisor has skills that make her powerful, restructure the units of accountability so the supervisor can grow and develop without being humiliated.

The growing power of computer technology can create bypassed supervisors and managers. A predicted impact of the computer is the leveling of organizations and the toppling of hierarchies. (Given that people have exercised power within hierarchies for at least the 5,000 years of recorded history, this prediction seems a mite overrated.) If databases and networks can give access to knowledge from all departments and all levels, traditional managers may be bypassed.

There are benefits to this development, of course—speed particularly. Rather than being subject to a time lag, decisions can be made in real time. If I supply parts to your company, you may not even have to tell me when stocks are low because I can pick up that information directly from your database. But how does accountability flow in this situation? Who delegates? How am I going to be held accountable? With certain businesses operating at such high speeds, there is a danger that I can do serious damage before you can catch up with me!

How?

People give accounts of their actions in very different ways and in very different styles. Among the most common methods of giving accounts in organizations are meetings, speeches, lectures, talks, memos, electronic mail, letters, and reports. Attentive managers never underestimate the significance of random encounters during breaks, in hallways, or by the coffee machine. Informal encounters are sometimes the only opportunity for a person to give an account of their work.

Giving an account may take the form of a test which is as much giving an account as sitting with someone and talking about their performance. Tests are not only written, they may be physical, for example, drug tests, AIDS tests, genetic tests, or polygraph tests. Many tests raise ethical and technical problems. Whatever the law says, random drug testing may simultaneously infringe individual liberty and raise the confidence of people who travel by train or plane. The polygraph may create illusion of certainty that is, in fact, unfounded.

When?

Accountability needs good timing. To make sure the *When?* criterion is operating properly, check:

Frequency.	Too often	v.	Not often enough
Regularity.	Regularly	v.	Irregularly
Timeliness.	Too early	v.	Too late

It is never too early to spell out the accountability mechanism, but do not demand the first account too early and make a decision to cancel a project or process without giving it a fair trial. The opposite danger is postponing the giving of an account and continuing to postpone it until you have invested so much money, time, effort, or prestige that what you are doing becomes impossible to stop. Psychologists call this sunk cost, entrapment, or escalation. In other words, your judgment is affected by how much you have already sunk into the enterprise. You are trapped on an ever ascending escalator of commitment.

Computers are forcing us to look at *When?* in a very different way. Take customer service. The combination of telephone and computer has led to greater convenience for customers, less waste, a greater opportunity for customized goods, and better quality service. But is there a danger of turning certain workplaces into electronic sweat shops? Nobody does numbers like computers. Everything a telephone representative does can be recorded. The time it takes to answer calls, to type in data, and to have a break can all be noted to a fraction of a second. It is possible that a representative need never give an account. The computer can do it by itself.

This raises the interesting question: Is it right to hold individuals accountable for every second—every nanosecond—of their working day? Your answer will be determined largely by two aspects of accountability I have already discussed: the danger of overaccountability and the choice between accountability values.

What if?

I shall comment only briefly on *What if?* as I shall be discussing it in detail later. The accountability mechanism forces you to ask whether sanctions exist, but it cannot tell you whether any sanctions that do exist are *appropriate*. There are times when other people will, in practice, make that decision for you: Congress, by passing a law, or senior management by issuing a policy. But many day-to-day decisions about sanctions are up to the individual manager's sense of right and wrong. *You* have to decide what is appropriate. Ask yourself: In situation *s*, what would be the minimum appropriate sanction, and what sanction would be totally unreasonable? In effect, another boundary question. Courts commonly define boundaries in this way, for example, by sending someone to prison for between six months and two years.

5

Responsibility

You have probably noticed the absence of the words "responsible" and "responsibility." This is deliberate. Often used interchangeably, accountability and responsibility have different meanings and different emphases. We can do much to improve accountability by carefully considering whether, in any given situation, accountability or responsibility conveys our meaning better.

Responsibility's Many Uses

First, unlike accountability, responsibility has many different uses. The word "responsible" can mean:

1. *The cause of something (and that is good)*

as in:

> "Yvonne is responsible for putting this conference together. Let's give her a hand!"

2. *The cause of something (and should be blamed)*

as in:

> "The architects are responsible for the poor design that led to the collapse of the building."

46   Accountability

3. *Knowing the difference between right and wrong.*

as in:

> "You're a responsible adult. Why did you do what was clearly wrong?"

4. *Trustworthy.*

as in:

> "Thelma is the most responsible person here, and I'm putting her in charge while I'm away."

5. *Having the duty to do something.*

as in:

> "You are responsible for getting the reports in on time."

6. *Having to explain yourself.*

as in:

> "You are responsible if things go wrong."

Meaning 6 is the one that most resembles accountability because you *may* have to explain yourself. But it is clearly not the same as accountability because to say, "You are responsible," does not confirm whether an account is actually to be given, or whether credible sanctions exist, if the account is unsatisfactory.

Different Emphases

The second difference between the words is that accountability emphasizes the link between the action and the consequences: responsibility emphasizes the link between the doer and the action. Put another way: "You are accountable" says a mechanism exists to hold you accountable. "You are responsible" is a statement of opinion or a moral judgement about what you have done. It may not result in sanctions or even having to give an account.

We can hold anyone responsible for anything, however ridiculous. I can hold you responsible for the weather, the failure of my favorite sports team, or the latest rise in interest rates. It is perfectly natural to hold people responsible because we all have opinions and make judgments. But holding people responsible does not improve things: holding people accountable does. With its lack of sanctions, responsibility is very much like, and is often the equivalent of, neutral accountability, and it can suffer from the same do-nothing paralysis I described when I distinguished neutral from strong accountability.

Since accountable and responsible have different meanings, we can be accountable for an action and not be responsible for it, and vice versa. Suppose I am employed by a business and work on a project for five days in a row at 20 hours a day. On the fifth day I make a serious mistake. I have to give an account of what happened and may be liable for sanctions. In that respect I am accountable. But if I am forced to work this way by my manager's poor planning, then I may not be held responsible in the sense of being blamed. Conversely, when something in an organization goes seriously or even criminally wrong only some people are forced to be accountable and sent to prison. Many more executives and managers were responsible for the Savings and Loan failures of the 1980s and early 1990s than were held accountable.

Or take a difficult, but all too common, example suggested by some earlier remarks. If it is true that we learn the basics of accountability at an early age; and if it is also true that some children are not exposed to these basics, how should we react if they commit a crime while still young? The law may ensure we hold them accountable, but are they the only ones responsible? To what extent should we hold others accountable, particularly their parents?

I realize I have painted a slightly critical and rather unusual picture of responsibility in this chapter, but I shall return to the word later in the book and describe the crucial role it plays in supporting accountability.

6

Direct and Visible Accountability

So far, I have described the accountability mechanism as if it were one-size-fits-all, and, in a way, this is true. The number of criteria and the shape of the units remain constant. But in another way we can say that accountability comes in different shapes and sizes. There are, if you like, different types or versions of the standard model. In this chapter and the next we shall examine the different versions. Here I shall distinguish between what I call direct and indirect, and visible and invisible accountability.

Direct and Indirect Accountability

The best way to distinguish between direct and indirect accountability is through an example. The CEO and board of a company are accountable to the shareholders—the owners. If the account they give is unsatisfactory, they can be fired. The CEO and the board get their authority directly from the shareholders; hence they are *directly* accountable. Direct accountability filters down from the shareholders through senior executives to managers and everyone else who works for the company. All employees are part of a chain of direct accountability and are, in effect, agents of the owners. Nearly all the examples I have discussed so far, the specialist, the manager, the salespeople, Louise, Dennis, Graham, Jim and Herb have been part of a direct accountability chain.

Some people are not part of the chain but, nevertheless, have a stake in the well-being of the organization. They are "stakeholders," and for a company they might be the suppliers who obviously need the company to prosper for their own financial success, or families in the local community who depend on the company for employment. The stakeholders too can hold the company accountable, but this type of accountability is *indirect* for two reasons. First, although they can strike, litigate, campaign, and boycott, stakeholders cannot employ the ultimate sanction and fire the CEO, the board, and individual managers. Second, although stakeholders may have the power to shape events, force managers to listen, or threaten to take the company to court, the authority invested in the management comes from the owners not the stakeholders.

You can try and make an organization indirectly accountable even if you are not an obvious stakeholder. If a musician releases a song which seems to condone attacks on the police, police unions can try to put pressure on investors to vote against the directors whose company released the song. Free speech apart, this is a clear example of indirect accountability.

The distinction between direct and indirect accountability is particularly important for managers in government services and nonprofits. Increasingly, the recipients of these services are described as customers. If this is to encourage good service, I am all for it, as long as we remember that customers—in the everyday sense of the word—have an element of choice. They can take their business elsewhere. The relationship between government and members of the public is different. Many government services are monopolies and monopolists do not have customers, they have dependents. If you are an immigrant you do not have a choice between competing immigration services. If you are a taxpayer there is only one federal tax collection service. Not every aspect of government has to be rigid, of course. Parents, given a choice of schools, can act more like customers.

If you work for a community-based, nonprofit organization and want to be accountable to those you are trying to help, you have to ask in what way you are linked to the helped, and what sanctions (apart from avoiding you) the helped really have. It is perfectly possible to do good work and still not be accountable to the beneficiaries of that work. Unless the targets of your goodwill and effort have real choices, you will not be accountable to them. You will, though, be the *Who?* in units where the donors and institutions who fund you are the *To?* There is, of course, nothing wrong with this, but we must clarify the relationship between accountability and trust as I shall in chapter 10.

Visible and Invisible Accountability

Up till now, we have only discussed accountability to flesh and blood human beings or to organizations, which comprise human beings. I call any instance when you are accountable to a person or a group *visible* accountability.

There are those, however, who claim to be accountable to invisible entities such as their principles or their consciences. *Invisible* accountability usually boils down to accountability to yourself, or accountability to your conscience. The criteria look something like this:

Who?	I
To?	My conscience
For?	My actions
How?	Thinking
When?	Either before or after I have acted
What if?	Guilt, anxiety, anguish

Is this real accountability? If you are happy with these answers, then it is. I am not. The mechanism is not specific enough for me: the sanctions too vague. Take accountability out of the domain of the physical world, away from flesh and blood human beings, and I doubt whether, in any practical sense, it continues to exist. If you make the more general point: I feel responsible for this action, you are giving me an opinion, or a description of your feelings, that I may or may not accept. The more concrete the mechanism of accountability, the easier it will be able to establish, discuss, and negotiate.

This is not to say people should not take values and beliefs into consideration when they act. Indeed, the discussion of accountability values showed this cannot be avoided. But asserting that values inevitably play a part in accountability is not the same as trying to juggle everyone's individual feelings. Accountability needs to be as public a process as possible.

A compromise might be that people are accountable to invisible entities if they act consistently as if they were accountable to them. We have to include "consistently" to overcome the temptation to pick and choose between principles. Presume, for a moment, I know you well. There are two principles I am certain you hold: (a) You oppose experiments on animals, and (b) You do not tolerate cheating. You are looking for a job and are offered a post in a biotech company that conducts tests on animals. You choose not to be accountable to principle (a) (oppose animal experiments) and take the job. You then discover major financial irregularities, decide to uphold principle (b) (not tolerate cheating), and blow the whistle on the company. You have chosen one principle and not another. Who am I to judge you? But if you claim to be accountable to your principles, I am entitled to ask: Which principle, exactly?

We can put these four types of accountability into a table. I am sure that the first concern of most managers will be visible and direct accountability, the more heavily shaded box,

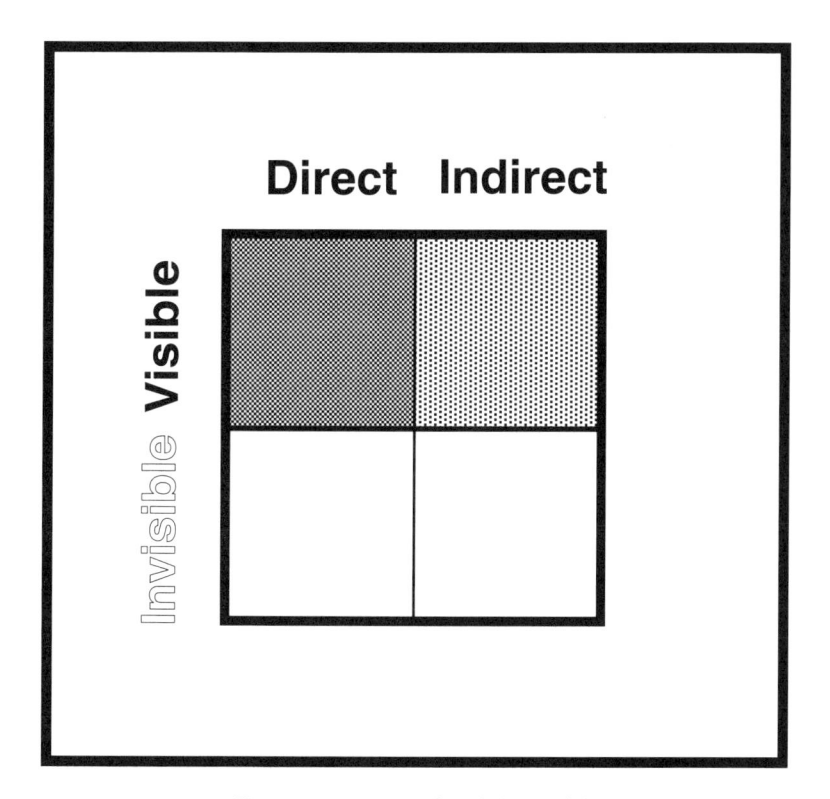

Fig. 6.1: Directness/Visibility Table

but visible, indirect accountability, the less heavily shaded box, may also have a bearing on their work.

7

More Types of Accountability

This chapter brings together three more issues essential to our understanding of accountability. First, I shall examine another contrasting pair of accountability types, official and personal accountability. Second, echoing the earlier discussion of style, I shall ask whether managers can or should be held accountable for the tone and direction they set. Third, I shall introduce two more accountability types, broad and narrow.

Personal and Official Accountability

An important distinction can be made between two more types of accountability, *personal* and *official*. I argued earlier that accountability is not the same as responsibility. But one thing they do have in common is the distinction between the personal use and the official use:

1. *Personal responsibility* means you are held responsible for what you, as an individual, do. You may have to justify yourself.

2. *Personal accountability* means that you are held accountable for what you, as an individual, do. The possibility of a sanction exists.

3. *Official responsibility* means that you are responsible for what is done by someone "below" you in your organization.

This responsibility exists whether you authorize the deed or not.

4. *Official accountability* means that you are held to account for the actions of others because of the position you hold. Again, the possibility of credible sanctions exists.

An example will show the difference between the terms. George commits an act of fraud against his company. Whether he is found out or not, he is *personally responsible*. If he is discovered and appropriate action is taken against him, he becomes *personally accountable*.

George's manager, Susan, is neither personally responsible nor personally accountable; but she is *officially responsible* because she oversees the area where the fraud has been committed. It has occurred in her department. In order for Susan to be held *officially accountable*, there needs to be the very real possibility that some sanction will be taken against her, for example, no promotion, moved to another department. The sanctions are likely to take effect if, when she gives her account of what happened, her carelessness or poor management are judged to have contributed to the fraud. If the consequences of George's actions are very serious, she may contemplate resigning.

However unfair this may seem, *being accountable for all actions "below" you comes with the territory of any management position*. Official accountability is what management is all about. Robert Albanese sums it up well when he says that accountability for the way people perform is the essence of the manager's job. The only reason we have management positions in the first place is to improve the performance of others.

Returning to Susan for a moment. Under what circumstances should she, or any manager, contemplate resigning?

Senior managers who have seriously mismanaged ought to resign, and, if they understand the meaning of the word "honor," resign with good grace. But the complex nature of many organizations makes it difficult to pin down where in the chain of accountability things have gone wrong, and corporations can be very good at covering their tracks.

But should managers resign even if they have not personally mismanaged? The case for this course of action is hard to argue in a "Don't blame me" age. Yet, in some countries, senior managers and politicians may resign even when the fault cannot be put at their door, as a *symbol* that something terrible has happened. Japan springs to mind, but the idea is not confined to a single culture. In 1982, for example, Argentina invaded the Falkland Islands, a British possession, and the British Foreign Secretary, Lord Carrington, resigned to acknowledge the enormity of the intelligence failure in his department even though it would be hard to blame him personally for this failure. Incidentally, this act did him no harm, as he went on to head NATO. In these circumstances, resignation is not just about blame, which would, of course, make it only an issue of responsibility.

At bottom, the question is this: *Can resignation be a symbolic act to acknowledge the seriousness of what has happened without necessarily implying that the person who resigns did wrong?* I do not see symbolic resignation becoming commonplace in the United States in the near future. Fear of the law and fear of blame are too strong. But it might create a greater sense of self-discipline and organizational discipline were the possibility at least on the table.

We must, though, raise a skeptical eyebrow at executives and politicians who "accept responsibility" when things go wrong, in the full knowledge that they will not be fired or forced to resign. Gail Collins has neatly described this growing tendency as "LoCal" responsibility.

Tone and Direction

Managers inevitably set the tone and direction for the organization as a whole or that part of it they manage. Although difficult to implement, the tone they set is something for which they ought to be held accountable. Suppose a manager exhorts his staff to be careful but is careless himself. How far should subordinates be held accountable for carelessness if they are simply emulating his style? No manager should be able to wriggle out of personal and official accountability by saying: I told people to be careful; if they weren't, that's not my fault. Or conversely, if he is cautious, but has told his staff to take risks, he should not be surprised if the staff too are cautious.

Managers' jobs are made up of the decisions they make and tone they set. A manager who encourages her staff to work right up to the legal limits of the job should never be able to evade accountability if one of them crosses the line and does something illegal. Everyone knows that the distinction between legal and illegal is often blurred. If you push people to the legal limit, there is a good chance they will overstep the line from time to time. In these circumstances, defending yourself by saying that you insisted that everyone work within the law and that you always assumed your instructions were followed should be insufficient.

If something goes wrong, your accountability may depend on the tone you set before the event occurred. Suppose a male manager has to handle an accusation of sexual harassment made by a female employee against a male member of staff in his department. He could start by having this conversation with himself:

Am I personally accountable?

No.

Will I be held officially accountable?

Yes, probably, given the policy in our company.

What action shall I take?

Get an account of what has happened and discipline the person if necessary.

What could I have done differently?

To answer the last question, he needs to ask another: Did this come as a surprise? Compare two managers, Allen and Bill. Allen has taken sexual harassment seriously in the past. He has discussed it with his staff, and issued clear policy guidelines. His conduct has demonstrated that he disapproves of sexual harassment and will take action against it. Bill seldom mentions sexual harassment. He thinks that, by not discussing it, he will never have to deal with it. When sexual harassment crops up elsewhere in the organization, he sends out a cursory memo. But in the privacy of his office he speaks disparagingly about women. When confronted by his assistant manager's good-natured banter, he accuses her, half in jest and half in fear, of harassing him.

The personal and the official accountability are identical but the tone and direction are very different. Allen cannot guarantee that sexual harassment will not occur in his section but he has set a tone that discourages it. Bill, on the other hand, has set a tone that, if not exactly encouraging sexual harassment, certainly indicates it is an issue way down on his scale of importance. So would harassment come as a surprise? In Allen's case, probably Yes: in Bill's, probably No. In any business or organization where accountability is taken seriously, senior staff will always be asking themselves: What tone am I setting? and What tone do my managers set?

If the staff of a company are guilty of corporate misdeeds, particularly financial ones, legal sanctions will depend on the tone that has been set. The company will be in a much stronger position if it has implemented a program that sets standards and procedures for its financial affairs; enforces those standards; and encourages employees to report financial irregularities without fear of retribution.

As you can see, this debate has many ramifications. Here is one more. Suppose a leader with a group of loyal followers fires them up to such an extent that one of them goes out and kills the leader's major opponent. The leader may defend himself by saying he gave no specific instructions for the opponent to be killed. But the tone of his oratory led in this direction and, given the loyalty of his followers, the death is neither unexpected nor unwelcome. Can, and should, we hold this leader accountable for the tone he sets?

Broad and Narrow Accountability

Individual managers, whatever their department or section, are part of one organization. Are there circumstances in which they should be held accountable not just for jobs done in their specific area but for the work of everyone in the organization? I have labeled this dichotomy *broad* and *narrow* accountability.

Broad accountability may, at first glance, seem to be overdoing things, but you can see the point in this example. Like me, you probably get irritated with this sort of exchange. You phone Juanita Gonzalez at work:

You:	Is Juanita Gonzalez there?
Them:	No.
You:	When will she be back?
Them:	Don't know.

No offer to take a message, no offer of help, no checking you have come through to the right department. At that particular moment, *the person answering the phone* is *the whole company* and they should be accountable at least for communicating effectively and civilly with the outside world whatever their position. It is not just a staff issue. Managers respond like this too.

What happens if the manager of another department is sick and you are the most senior manager around? Don't you have some obligation to see that things are operating reasonably in the other manager's absence? Is this only responsibility or should you be held accountable? If we employ the accountability criteria, which should always be our instinctive reaction when we are uncertain, we can see immediately where the difficulties lie. For example, should sanctions be taken against managers who do not take initiative? As professionals, aren't managers automatically accountable for a broader range of actions than their immediate jobs? The criteria of the mechanism, in combination with boundary questions, should be our first step towards clearing up these difficulties.

It is fitting that we are ending this chapter by returning to the accountability criteria once again. The criteria are at the heart of the mechanism which, in turn, is at the heart of accountability. But we must always keep in mind that the mechanism comes in different shapes or types which we have discussed in this and the previous chapter.

Direct	and	Indirect
Visible	and	Invisible
Personal	and	Official
Broad	and	Narrow

62   Accountability

To see how these different ways of viewing accountability come together, I shall integrate them into a case study of a well-known accident.

8

The Challenger *Accident*

The first seven chapters outlined what accountability is and how it works. To be as clear as I could, I made the examples and tips short and general, so they would not hold up the flow of explanation. Before going on, I want to demonstrate the importance of my subject more emphatically by examining an event where accountability turned out to be a matter of life and death. I shall describe the events leading to the loss of the space shuttle *Challenger* on January 28, 1986 and then offer a number accountability lessons which relate directly to points I have made so far.

Background

The shuttle program was approved in the early 1970s during the Nixon administration. The big-spending days of the Apollo moon-landing program were over, and new space initiatives would have to be realized with smaller budgets. The package of hardware that left the launch pad every mission—the shuttle itself, an external fuel tank and two rocket boosters (Fig. 8.1)—would, in the main, have to be reusable. A fleet of shuttles was needed to ensure that launches would be regular, commercial, and, therefore, cost-effective. If these conditions had not been promised by the National Air and Space Administration (NASA), it is unlikely there would have been a shuttle program.

64   Accountability

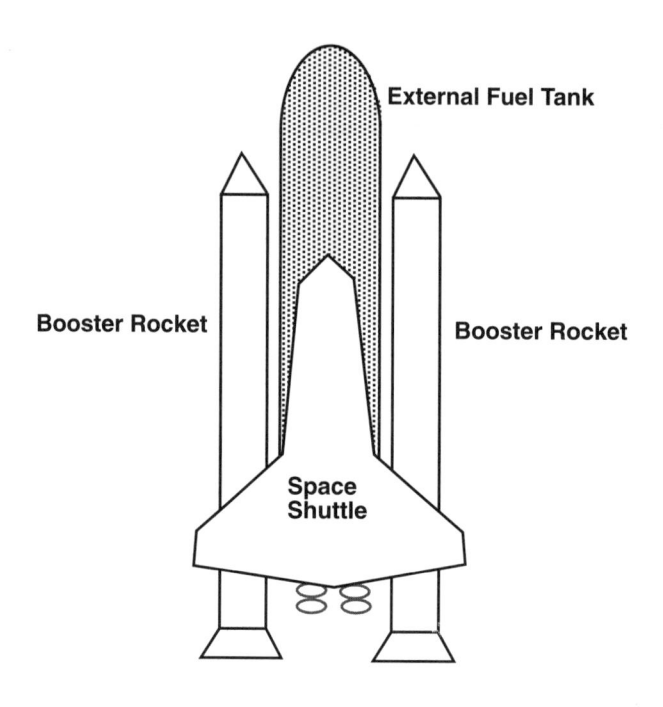

Fig. 8.1: What Leaves the Launch Pad

The contract for the solid rocket boosters was awarded to the Utah-based company Thiokol which had become Morton Thiokol Inc. (MTI) by the time of the *Challenger* accident. According to the criteria set by NASA, Thiokol was not the number one choice. The Lockheed design scored better, but Thiokol was chosen because their design cost less than Lockheed's and NASA considered the Thiokol management structure more effective.

Unlike the one-piece design suggested by another competitor, Thiokol had designed their booster rocket in parts for easier transportation. But this approach demanded an assurance that the parts would fit together exactly and would not break up when the rocket was launched. The joints had to hold firm and seal properly.

Booster Rocket Problems

The booster rockets were plagued with trouble almost from the start. These problems became worse after the shuttle program got underway in 1983. The nagging doubt was this: How effective, and therefore, how safe, were the joints (the so-called "field joints") between the different segments of the booster rockets once they had been assembled at the launch site—the Kennedy Space Center, Florida?

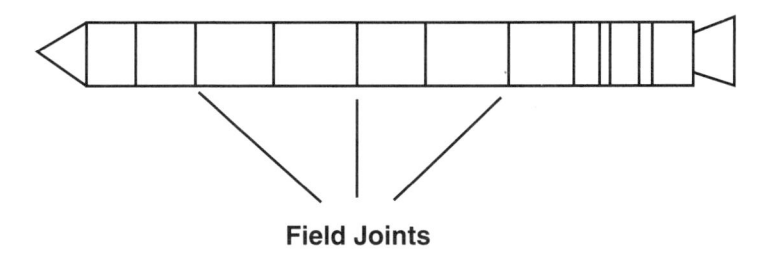

Fig. 8.2: Booster Rocket

Two rubber seals called O-rings were important components in each joint. When the booster rockets were examined, following their recovery from the sea after every launch, the O-rings often appeared to be damaged. This damage had not led to the destruction of the shuttles involved and became accepted by certain NASA decision makers as part of the wear and tear of shuttle launching even though damage to the O-rings *could* lead to the loss of a mission because, if things went wrong, there was no backup for these parts. In NASA-speak, the O-rings were not redundant.

The O-ring doubts continued into 1985 when engineers at MTI expressed such concern that a special seal team was set up to make a concerted effort to overcome the problems. By January 1986, however, they had still not finished conducting their tests.

Challenger Launch

These problems remained unknown to the public at large. As far as ordinary Americans were concerned, everything was going fine. The *Challenger* flight was another routine shuttle mission, the twenty-sixth. It was so routine that the crew included a New Hampshire teacher, Christa McAuliffe, who was going to give lessons from space.

After delays, the launch of the *Challenger* was set for January 28. The day before the launch, the engineers at MTI were particularly concerned that the very low temperatures expected for the next day would damage the O-rings. The lowest temperature at which a shuttle had been launched up till then was 53° F and there had been significant O-ring damage on that occasion. It was likely the temperature would be 20° below this. At about 9 p.m. EST, a telephone conference call (a telecon, in NASA jargon) took place between people involved in the project at three different locations: (a) Kennedy Space Center in Florida, (b) Marshall Space Flight Center in Alabama and (c) MTI Headquarters in Utah. MTI engineers argued that it was too risky to launch. NASA officials were displeased, but MTI management backed the engineers. At the end of the telecon it looked as though the launch would be postponed, but NASA wanted final written confirmation of that recommendation.

The discussion continued in Utah. No one was positively pro-launch, but a significant shift took place in management thinking. The managers, as opposed to the engineers, recommended a launch in the absence of firm data that the launch would not be safe.

There were a few last minute attempts to delay the launch, and it was so cold that a considerable amount of ice had to be removed in the early morning. But the launch went ahead. During the 73 seconds of the mission, hot gas escaped through a booster rocket "field joint" which led to the rupturing of the fuel tank and a catastrophic explosion. None of the seven astronauts survived. The accident was investigated both by a presidential commission (the Rogers Commission, named after its chairman, William Rogers) and by the United States Congress.

Accountability Lessons

1. *The failure of just one accountability criterion can have serious repercussions.*

The *Who?* criterion was not operational at the start of the crucial telecon (telephone conference) the night before the launch. Telecons were very common forums for communication since the NASA centers of operation and their contractors were scattered throughout the United States. It was a rule of the telecon that all participants had to identify themselves before the meeting began. On this occasion, the rule was broken, which turned out to be significant.

Two managers at the MTI end of the conference did not identify themselves, so the conferees at the two NASA centers did not know exactly who was giving the account. If you had been at one of the NASA centers, you would probably have thought: This telecon is mostly with engineers, so we are going to arrive at a purely engineering decision. When MTI changed its mind later in the evening, you might reasonably have supposed an engineering recommendation—as opposed to a management recommendation—had been made. Your view of the launch might have been very different had you been aware that a group of managers had made the final recommendation in opposition to the engineering consensus.

2. *Defining the accountability borders can be difficult.*

After the telecon between MTI and the two NASA centers, the borders defining what the MTI engineers were accountable for subtly changed. Normally the contractors were accountable for the decision to fly. In effect, they had to affirm that their machinery was going to work. On this particular evening, the policy seemed to be reversed, and they became accountable for the decision not to fly—in other words, they had to prove the shuttle was *not* safe.

In our daily lives, proving a negative is practically impossible. In the case of *Challenger*, the data were suggestive but not conclusive. MTI couldn't prove absolutely that the rocket wouldn't work.

3. *Accountability values, in this case risk versus safety, are an integral part of the* For? *criterion.*

The success of the moon landing program and the establishment of the shuttle program created a pervasive attitude throughout NASA of not merely "can do" but "can't fail." "Can't fail" means the shuttle was as safe as a commercial airliner and certainly safe enough to send a teacher into space. So good was the shuttle that it had been declared "operational" after only four flights!

But a shuttle is not as safe as a commercial airliner. Manned space flight is always going to be dangerous and risky; but take no risks and it will cease. Once you have decided to undertake a program with clear dangers, you must still continue to ask: What are the odds involved? NASA should be able to make this imaginary assertion to astronauts every time they board a shuttle: We have considered all the risks to this venture and we have concluded that (a) there are no foreseeable problems with the hardware, (b) we have done some serious estimation of the general risks involved with the hardware and we think they are tolerable, and (c) we have reduced as much as possible the number of items for which there is no backup.

Even with a dangerous task, you can encourage playing it safe rather than risk-taking.

In the case of *Challenger* these statements could not have been made. (a) The O-ring problem was foreseeable and foreseen. (b) Rogers Commissioner, Richard Feynman, in an appendix to the Commission's report, said he had found a wide range of estimates regarding the chances of one of the three main shuttle engines failing (not the booster rockets with the O-rings). The manufacturer's engineers had one estimate, 1 in 10,000; NASA engineers at the Marshall Space Center had another estimate, 1 in 300, and NASA management had another estimate, 1 in 100,000. A considerable discrepancy in risk estimation! (c) Over 700 items were listed as Criticality 1 (no redundancy) and waivers to fly with these items had to be signed by the person in charge of launching. The O-rings had been designated Criticality 1 for a number of years but a waiver was signed (as it had been on six previous shuttle flights) even though NASA was aware of the problems MTI were having with the seals. It was as though NASA assumed that every time a launch was successful this somehow made things safer.

So taking these points together, the bias of this accountability value dilemma which should have been in favor of playing safe was, in practice, in favor of risk-taking—not surprising for a "can't fail" organization.

4. *Accountability can go haywire when the* Who? *and* To? *are not clearly differentiated.*

A change of "slots" occurred on the evening before the launch. After the telecon had finished and people at MTI were moving towards a decision whether to recommend a launch or not, one of the engineers, who had a management position as well, was told by the senior manager present to take off his engineering hat and put on his management hat. In other words he moved from being part of the *Who?* (engineers) to being part of the *To?* (management). It became clear during the testimony to the Rogers Commission that this affected the decision-making process and contributed to the pro-launch recommendation.

An engineer's job is different from a manager's. In this case, the job of the engineer should be to measure risk; the job of the manager should be to judge the acceptability of risk. People should not suddenly swap hats to justify decisions.

5. *It is up to individuals to decide whether they are accountable to their consciences.*

How hard it is to be accountable to oneself, one's conscience, or one's principles—invisible accountability—can easily be grasped by asking the question: Should the MTI engineers have considered themselves accountable to their consciences and done more to stop the launch? What more should they have done? It is hard to go against management before an action is taken, and whistle blowing after the event is tough, as a senior seal engineer found to his cost when he made public how unhappy the engineers had been about the O-rings. He was ostracized and eventually had to go on sick leave.

It was clear by 1985 that the seal problem needed to be rectified. The engineers working on the seals knew the danger and did not remain silent. A memo written in July 1985 by one of the engineers suggested that a team dedicated to solving the seal problem be put together, or else a flight might be lost. Despite this memo and others, the work of the seal team was delayed.

One reason I am hesitant to treat invisible accountability as full accountability is that if more attention had been paid to the mechanism of visible accountability, the pressure put on individual consciences would not have been so great. One group of commentators has observed that individuals should not have to be moral heroes. More time should have been spend on creating structures in which staff could act ethically. Having said that, there is simply no system that will produce a "right" answer in a case like this. Even if the accountability links had been better spelled out, there are some decisions that revolve around the personality of the individuals concerned. Who can say that any of us in their position would have acted any differently?

6. *Accountability is not the same as responsibility. Although you can hold almost anyone responsible for some events, it requires much more to hold people accountable.*

To appreciate the vagueness of responsibility, simply ask: Who was responsible for the *Challenger* disaster? Even the brief background summary suggests all sorts of places where the responsibility might lie. We could blame individuals: the NASA manager responsible for the launch; the MTI manager who signed off on the decision to launch the night before; MTI managers who did not take the seals problems seriously enough; the head of NASA for not running a "tight ship"; the MTI engineers for not fighting harder for their views. We could blame organizations: the Nixon administration for being too cheap; NASA for being too ambitious; MTI for not investigating the seal problem properly; Congress for not keeping closer safety tabs on NASA; the public for not continuing to show enough interest in the space program.

7. *If official accountability is to work, there needs to be a clear definition of appropriate sanctions.*

NASA did not take strong action against senior managers after the disaster. It was almost like musical chairs. One commentator has remarked that none were terminated or even publicly castigated. Some took voluntary retirement; some received lateral transfers; and some even remained in their positions. The point is that you cannot just do anything and call it a sanction. Sanctions must be credible and commensurate with the absence of the action/consequence relationship. In the case of *Challenger*, the sanctions were neither credible nor commensurate. Official accountability should have prevented senior managers from pleading ignorance or pretending they had nothing to do with the events.

8. *The tone senior managers set can create real dangers for an organization.*

The tone set by senior managers at NASA influenced the actions of more junior managers. One reason sanctions did not seem to be taken seriously was that failure was not expected. It had been nearly twenty years since the Apollo 1 fire which had taken the lives of three astronauts. Since then there had been six successful moon landings, a dramatic space rescue (Apollo 13), and a number of other high profile ventures. As I said earlier, in the early days of NASA, the tone set by senior managers was "can do." By the time the shuttle program was underway, these successes had bred another tone—"can't fail." If you believe you are not going to fail, the idea of accountability becomes less relevant, and the mechanism atrophies. Senior NASA managers ignored what the ancient Greeks understood only too well: hubris—an exaggerated self-confidence that often results in retribution.

This exaggerated self-confidence spread down the organization. Junior managers tended to have a very positive view of the organization and were not afraid to take responsibility. (Whether they were accountable or not, is, of course, quite another matter.) After all, if it was a "can't fail" organization, then it was almost ideal. As Howard Schwartz put it, in a psychoanalytic perspective of the disaster, if the tone that is set is of a flawless organization, there may be a built-in tendency to take too much responsibility and act too positively.

9. *Competition between different units of accountability can distort one's perspective.*

Like any CEO, the CEO of MTI was accountable to the owners (i.e. the shareholders) of his company for making a profit, and to his customers, in this case NASA, for a properly working product. People in charge of companies are always in this central server position, but how they handle their predicament will depend on their personalities. With the remains of the astronauts quite recently interred, and the future of the shuttle program in doubt, one might have forgiven MTI's CEO had he trodden gingerly when his accountability to the shareholders was raised in an interview with the *Wall Street Journal*. But No. He fearlessly commented that the accident would cost "only 10¢ a share."

10. *In the interests of organizational accountability, it is sometimes right for senior executives to heed the advice of managers trying to accept broad responsibility.*

An MTI manager at the Kennedy Space Center was so opposed to the launch that, even when the go-ahead had been given, he took the view that he was responsible for more than his department and continued to try and reverse the decision with other arguments. He maintained that, in addition to the cold O-rings, the sea was too rough for the ships recovering the booster rockets, and the formation of ice on the *Challenger* would be a problem. But, in the end, even he was defeated. He reported to the Rogers Commission that he was told he shouldn't concern himself with these matters.

Conclusion

The uncertainty of life precludes any absolute statement such as: "If they had only done this, then the *Challenger* disaster could have been averted." An understanding of organizational flux should counteract any such smugness. But I think we can reasonably conclude that had accountability been properly understood and acted upon before the launch, *Challenger* might very well not have been lost. Certainly, a very different accident could have occurred as when, at a previous launch, 18,000 pounds of liquid oxygen was drained accidentally from the external fuel tank of the shuttle *Columbia* five minutes before lift-off. The countdown was stopped just in time.

But paying attention to accountability improves the odds against a mishap, not just in the space program but in every single organization because these lessons have general application. A tribute we can all pay to the brave men and women who died in the accident is to apply the lessons of the tragedy to our daily working lives.

Part Two

Let's now examine accountability anew but with different questions. Instead of asking: "What is accountability?" "How does it work?" and "How can we repair it?" we are going to ask: "What right have we to hold accountable?" and "When should accountability apply?" Chapters 9 and 10 give provisional answers to these questions which are fleshed out through examples in chapters 11 to 14. Parts One and Two are summarized in chapter 15.

9

Legitimacy

This book aims to demonstrate the assertion that accountability is a vital part of all organizations. But even if you agree we are faced with additional questions: What right do we have to hold anybody accountable in the first place? What is behind accountability? Accountability is underwritten by the belief that to hold people accountable is reasonable, rightful, and lawful or, put another way, legitimate. *Accountability is underwritten by legitimacy.* So where does legitimacy come from? Let's go exploring!

The Legitimacy River

Suppose we are standing on the bank of the Mississippi River a few miles upstream from where it flows into the Gulf of Mexico. By this stage, it has been fed by hundreds, probably thousands, of tributaries and I cannot point to a particular square foot of water and say: "That 'bit' of water comes from the Ohio River. The 'bit' in front of it comes from the Yellowstone River," and so on. The water from the different rivers is all mixed up.

We can, though, go upriver and explore the river system and its sources. Some of the sources are obvious, a lake or a spring. Some are harder to identify, for example, an area of marshy ground. Occasionally, we can make out water from a particular source if it disgorges an unusual amount of silt or pollution into the Mississippi. The river may be of two colors

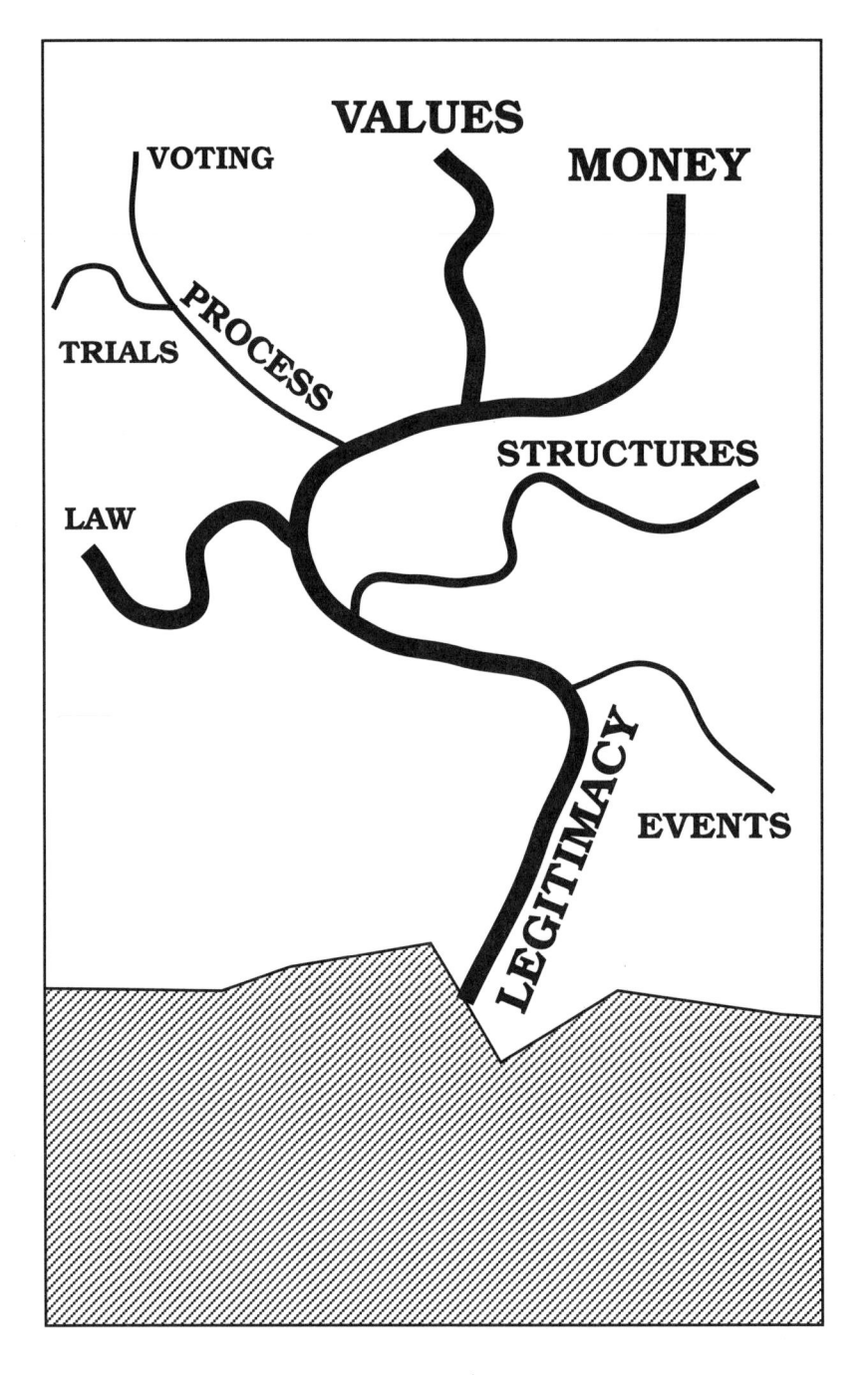

Fig. 9.1: Legitimacy River System

for a few miles. Eventually, though, the water from the two rivers will become completely blended.

Legitimacy is like a great river, and the Legitimacy River has important parallels with the Mississippi.

1. Many different tributaries go to make up legitimacy. We shall examine the main ones in a moment.

2. We can trace these tributaries of legitimacy to their sources. One obvious example is the law. I can hold you accountable when the law gives me the right to do so.

3. Certain sources are easy to identify, others are not. Religious texts and secular laws are used to hold people accountable. When these are insufficient, we have to fall back on general concepts like freedom or equality.

4. Accountability in our daily lives is derived from different sources of legitimacy and it may very well appear "mixed up."

5. Some tributaries play a greater role than others, but all make a contribution. After all, the word con*tribut*ion has the same root as the word *tribut*ary.

The Legitimacy River differs from the Mississippi in one important respect. The Mississippi rises independently of other rivers and would continue to exist, although in a much diminished condition, even if the other rivers stopped feeding into it. Legitimacy, however, does not exist independently of its sources. Those sources give us the justification to hold people accountable. They are constantly evolving and many of them, through tradition, have become so much part of our lives that they are hard to make out individually.

Here are some of the most important sources:

Values. The values and morals of every society are rooted in tradition but change over time. The identifiable sources are often sacred books, but these are subject to commentary, reinterpretation, and adaptation in the face of increasing scientific knowledge and social and technological forces.

The Legitimacy River explains why two values that, individually, meet with general approval can actually be in conflict. They have different sources. Do parents have the right to instill their values into their children? Yes. Do people have the right to their opinions? Yes. At what age does a young person's individual rights supersede her family's rights? A tough call. Family rights and personal rights come from different sources.

Laws. Some, although not all, of our values are codified in constitutions, laws, regulations, directives, orders, et cetera. The fact that they are written down and in the public domain means, of course, we are able to spend a lot of time arguing about them.

Process. The way we do certain things may be a source of legitimacy. In democracies, the electorate's act of voting and its ability to change legislators is the rationale for obeying laws and obeying the government. The act of putting your case before twelve jurors and the act of signing a contract also create legitimacy.

Events. Events in a country's history create legitimacy. In the case of the United States, the success of the Revolution legitimized the actions of The People. The Declaration of Independence begins "We the people...," and when politicians want to pep up their speeches, they assert that The People will, or won't, approve of such and such a measure. Revolution and gaining independence are powerful legitimizing events in many countries and their importance is celebrated on "national days"—July 4, in the United States, July 14, in France, May 5, in Mexico, et cetera.

Structures. The structures of society are a source of legitimacy. For example, it is reasonable for children to be accountable to their parents because the family structure, whatever its shape and size, is part of society's accountability chain. Businesses, government, and voluntary organizations are all structures that have become legitimate over time.

Money. Money is so important in nearly every society that it needs to be treated as a separate source of legitimacy. I said earlier that the acts of voting and revolution were sources of legitimacy. Similarly, the act of exchanging money automatically makes a transaction legitimate unless you can discover a good reason—for example, the money has been stolen—to override the legitimacy. The paper of the dollar bill with which I buy a loaf of bread is intrinsically worthless. But the baker and I agree that the exchange is legitimate using the equation: 1 portrait of George Washington = 1 loaf. And, because I give the baker that particular portrait, we both agree I have the right to hold him accountable if the loaf is in any way defective.

For some people, money has become the only real legitimacy and the cut and thrust of business the only reality. This is, presumably, why they call the business world the "real world," as if everything else were unreal. Money is indeed a mighty tributary of the Legitimacy River, but there is a danger in seeing it as the only one. If this were the case, then the actions of buying a loaf, buying a vote, buying a share in a company, and buying a hostage's freedom would be morally and emotionally indistinguishable. In practice, we view these four purchases differently, so other sources must be having an impact on our thinking.

A few words of caution here. I have not identified all the sources of legitimacy, but I am sure these six would be in most people's "top ten." Just because I have identified the sources, it does not mean that we all have to approve of them. The point is to recognize them. It is unlikely that you and I will completely agree on the order of importance of the different sources because our life experience is different. And we must always remind ourselves that legitimacy sources can contradict one another.

Once the major sources have been identified, we can use them to further clarify the operation of the accountability mechanism. Here are some examples.

Competition between Sources

The very first unit of accountability we examined was that of the specialist and the manager in which the specialist is accountable to the manager for doing an agreed job satisfactorily. Suppose you ask a specialist why she agrees to be accountable to her manager, Kate, you might get responses which are derived from different legitimacy sources:

> "I'm paid to do the job" *means* I have exchanged my labor for money (money legitimacy).

> "I've got a contract with the company" *means* I have committed the act of signing a contract and the law will protect me (process and law legitimacy).

> "Well, Kate's my boss, isn't she?" *means* I accept the right of my manager to tell me what to do (structure legitimacy).

> "Kate treats me well" *means* Kate demonstrates honesty and support (values legitimacy).

To repeat: When figuring out people's legitimacy mixes, you do not have to agree with every argument they make. What is important is that you recognize where the responses are coming from. In practice, managers often have to handle competition between their own legitimacy mix and the legitimacy mixes of those they manage.

Competition within Sources

Competition exists *within* sources as well as between them—law against law, value against value. Competition is not necessarily a life and death struggle. It is often more like achieving precedence by elbowing other sources out of the way. Which of two legal rulings or which of two values should take precedence? *Challenger* provided a more serious example of a conflict arising from one source: money. We saw how the CEO of Morton Thiokol was a central server officially accountable to both the customer, NASA, and to the shareholders. The customers paid him to make rockets: the shareholders paid him to make profits. One explanation of his seemingly callous observation about the price of the shares (page 75) is simply that he decided that the shareholders' unit of accountability took precedence over the customers'.

Competition also arises when water from a new source (often related to an old one) tries to become part of the Legitimacy River. The civil rights movement and the women's movement have ensured that it is reasonable and legitimate for an organization to aim to be diverse. This struggle was not won overnight and it continues today. Diversity has to counter other values and other sources of legitimacy. Shouldn't employers be free to employ whomever they want? Aren't men and women already treated equally in the eyes of the law? Shouldn't people be allowed to make money in whatever way they see fit? Remember, though, we are talking about precedence. No answers can make the aim of diversity "wrong."

Direct and Indirect Accountability Revisited

In the discussion of direct and indirect accountability (chapter 6), I said that direct accountability derives from the owners' ability to fire the CEO. The stakeholders can influence the owners' decisions but cannot make them. That is why accountability to stakeholders is indirect. By adding the different sources of legitimacy, the distinction between the groups becomes even more pronounced. Roughly speaking, the owners' legitimacy mix is this:

Shares and property
(money)

+

The traditional activities of corporation
(structures)

+

Voting for office holders
(process)

The stakeholders' legitimacy mix is (approximately) this:

The rights of The People to protest
(events)

+

The use of the law
(law)

+

A fair hearing for them and their families
(values and structure)

The two mixes are in constant competition. This competition is only a special example of the wider struggle between two valid sources of legitimacy, money and procedure; or as one set of combatants prefers to call it: free enterprise v. government regulation.

In the original discussion of direct and indirect accountability, I said that the ultimate sanction the shareholders can take against the CEO is to fire him. This is supported by the owners' legitimacy which I described above. But the CEO can to be held accountable through other legitimacy mixes. For example, if he is accused of financial wrong doing, the Security and Exchange Commission (SEC) may want to hold him accountable. The SEC's legitimacy mix comprises a different structure (the government), a different set of laws, and perhaps a different way of looking at the values of doing right and avoiding wrong.

Legitimacy and Invisible Accountability

Let me reiterate my view that invisible accountability and its most common manifestation, being accountable to oneself, is not real accountability. My reservations are twofold: first, I don't believe true sanctions are involved; second, accountability is about the relationship between flesh and blood people, not the relationship between conflicting feelings inside the heads of individuals.

It is certainly true that we may well have different views of accountability because we have different views of the importance of the main sources of legitimacy. But that is not the same as saying that there is a source of legitimacy that is special to me as an individual, and you cannot understand or discuss it. Since no individual has a privileged perspective of legitimacy, accountability to oneself simply boils down to this: Certain sources of legitimacy are important to me. The rest I ignore.

Here is the difficulty. If it were true that people had personal sources of legitimacy, then anyone could say: What I do is legitimate, because I say so; and if you don't recognize it, tough! Some people get away with this, of course. Charismatic leaders say: Forget the other sources of legitimacy, do what *I* say. Such people count themselves as sources of legitimacy, and if they get enough followers, they do indeed become, over time, an accepted source. A little caution is not unreasonable in the face of such claims, however attractive the individuals may be.

The Need for Sources of Legitimacy

"Power tends to corrupt," wrote Lord Acton, "and absolute power corrupts absolutely." There is always a danger that the more power a person has, the more cavalierly they will treat legitimacy. But, because you have power and can force people to do your will, it does not follow that the people you coerce have to accept your power as legitimate. And, if they don't accept your legitimacy, they won't feel accountable though they may feel something else, threatened, perhaps. Forcing people to give an account, but ignoring the standard sources of legitimacy, is power masquerading as accountability. Dictators understand this well and often spend an unusual amount of time justifying themselves in terms of traditional legitimacy: "I took power in the name of the Country, The People, Fighting Corruption, Justice, Tradition," and so on.

What applies to dictators applies in our everyday lives. If you try and hold accountable those you manage and they are unable to trace the source of your legitimacy, they will consider your attempts as unfair and oppressive. We must constantly seek the sources because *accountability without legitimacy is no longer accountability.*

A Note on Ethics

The Legitimacy River explains why business ethics is such a fraught area. Some of the legitimacy tributaries do not mix very well together. Here is an example of a common problem. When the president and vice president of a certain large company were jailed and fined for corporate wrongdoing, no one had predicted this turn of events. For example, the vice president was known as a figure of propriety and rectitude. He was a fixture in the local church and active in the community. The assumption here is that when the money tributary and the values tributary meet, their waters will mix together without difficulty. They won't. The financial pressure of the "real world" may overwhelm the moral pressure. Since the sources are separate, it is certainly possible that someone who, on Sunday, is a fixture in the local church, may, on Monday, overstep the legal boundaries at work in his attempt to be accountable to "money legitimacy." There is no reason to assume that morals, beliefs, and behavior learned outside the workplace are somehow *automatically* imported into the workplace.

Despite cases like this, the good news is that every day people are using their judgment to work ethically, balance the competing sources, and negotiate mixes of legitimacy that are good for them and good for all the units of accountability of which they are a part.

To summarize the message of this chapter: The right to hold people accountable derives from a mix of different sources of legitimacy. We tackled accountability problems by identifying individual units of accountability. In the same way, we can tackle legitimacy problems by identifying different sources.

10

Trust

It has been a recurring theme of this book that to strengthen accountability we must tighten its meaning. But we cannot tighten accountability simply by tightening legitimacy. If you glance at the Legitimacy River map again, you will realize that a huge number of actions can be considered legitimate, and we must face the inevitable fact that *there are more actions we consider legitimate than we can, in practice, hold people accountable for*. The position looks like this:

Fig. 10.1: Accountability and Legitimate Actions

It is not just too many actions. Sometimes we deliberately avoid making people accountable. For example, it is very difficult to hold accountable justices on the Supreme Court—and that is intentional. We do not want them to be accountable to politicians and other interest groups. We value their independence. We accept their actions as legitimate because we hope they will act in a disinterested way.

Responsibility Revived

If we cannot hold justices accountable, we have to *trust* them to do a good job. This is where responsibility really comes into its own. In chapter 5, I identified the following characteristics of responsibility: it has many meanings; it is a matter of judgment; it is different from accountability; and it cannot make people accountable. In everyday use, the different meanings of responsible fall under two headings: *cause* and *obligation*:

You are responsible	= 1. *Cause*	= You did wrong (blame)
		= You did well (praise)
		= You must answer
	= 2. *Obligation*	= You know your duty
		= You are trustworthy
		= You know right and wrong

There is no reason why the two main meanings cannot appear in the same sentence: Rob is responsible for doing the calculations, and he is responsible for most of the mistakes that occur. First use, obligation: second use, cause.

The cause meanings were my target earlier because those are the meanings most often confused with accountability. They are the meanings that allow people to get away without sanctions. But when we have to evaluate legitimate-but-can't-hold-accountable actions, we have to draft the obligation meaning of responsibility into service. I did this a moment ago by saying we have to trust Supreme Court justices. In fact, we have to rely on the trustworthiness of so many individuals that lawyers use the word *trustee* to designate such people. The legal use of the term—one who is trusted to look after another's property—has now grown to mean anyone we have to trust to look after public matters.

We want trustees not only to be trustworthy but to have an idea of duty and know the difference between right and wrong. They should act in a way that demonstrates they understand all the obligation meanings of the word responsible. So responsibility needs to be encouraged not just because of its intrinsic moral worth but because it has a job to do. *Responsibility reaches actions accountability can't reach*. We have to rely on responsibility when we can no longer rely on accountability. If we cannot agree on general guidelines concerning what actions are responsible and what are not, then whether "we" are a family, a business, or society, we are in trouble. We are back to boundary questions again.

Deliberate Trust

We can make good use of the fact that the word "trustee" has taken on a more general meaning. Trustees are not confined to society's big hitters like judges, politicians, or senior executives. I am sure that everyone can think of an occasion when they should have been held accountable but weren't.

When this happens, we automatically become trustees. We may not be trustees in a legal sense, but we are trustees in a practical sense. It follows that trust may exist "by accident" whether we plan to trust someone or not. Or put another way: If we cannot, or do not, hold people accountable, what choice do we have but to trust them? If I am not holding you accountable, I am trusting you, even if it has never crossed my mind to do so; even if I think you are the most untrustworthy person on the planet!

We can improve this unpalatable state of affairs by being very deliberate in the way we trust. Here are some examples.

1. When we ask people to pay on an honor system, we have made a specific choice to trust them.

2. A nominee to the Supreme Court goes through a Senate confirmation hearing and if he or she gets a majority of the vote, the Senate is in fact saying: We have chosen to trust you to uphold the Constitution. Given the political jockeying that surrounds Supreme Court nominations, such uprightness may be hard to believe! But in simple terms that is what the vote says. Again, a deliberate act of trusting.

3. Some managers feel that to trust people is to make them better employees, so they aim to reach a halfway house between accountability and trust. They deliberately ease off on daily accountability by checking less. Sanctions still exist, and the manager knows that if anything goes wrong he, as the manager, remains officially accountable. But if the job gets done better or faster, the risk of things going wrong is worth taking. The manager may be doing both himself and the employee a favor by moving away from the stress of excessive over-accountability.

4. The more deliberate the trust, the more severe the repercussions should be for abusing it. Lawyers recognized this hundreds of years ago when they took the Latin word for "to trust"—*fidere*—and turned it into the word "fiduciary," meaning a solemn legal trust. There is nothing casual about fiduciary relationships which include the trust placed in CEOs by shareholders and the trust placed in attorneys by their clients. If we are trusted as fiduciaries, we must act in the interest of others even when this interferes with our own interest. The message of the law is this: If you are the one trusted in a fiduciary relationship, you had better not take advantage of that trust or you will suffer severe consequences. Because this is often hard to implement (as we shall see in chapter 13), "fiduciary" is often linked to the word "duty." And duty, as a subdivision of obligation, is something we have to rely on when accountability is weak.

If we treat trust as something that requires a deliberate choice, e.g., an honor system, a process, delegation, fiduciary duty, we have to *think*. But, as I said earlier, situations of trust may arise whether we think about them or not. We can contrast deliberate trust with its careless cousin, "thoughtless" trust. Thoughtless trust occurs when people are short of time, don't understand what trust really means, or can't be bothered to think through what is happening around them. You may have problems of thoughtless trust if you find yourself saying things like this:

You: *I assumed you had done it.*
    Don't assume anything.

You: *I expect you to act like a professional.*
    What is your definition of professional?

You: *When something goes wrong, you should tell me at once.*

Every little thing?

You: *Why wasn't I informed?*

What is it about you that people won't tell you things?

You: *Can't anyone do anything right around here?*

Yes, actually, they can; but sometimes they make mistakes.

In short: when you're not checking, you're trusting!

If you look at the diagram at the beginning of this chapter, you will see that the boundaries of the accountability circle are sharp. More accurately, the edge is blurred:

Fig. 10.2: Accountability Frontier

Why? It's competition again. But this time, it exists between what people are held accountable for and what they aren't. There are two competitions going on here: one to do with ethics, the other with power. The ethical competition concerns this question: "Here are the sum total of legitimate actions; which *should* we hold people accountable for and which shouldn't we?" The power competition question is phrased slightly differently: "Here are the sum total of legitimate actions; which *can* we hold people accountable for and which can't we." Combine these questions with what we actually *do* hold people accountable for and we have a new way of looking at accountability. For example, to return a final time to members of the Supreme Court:

Should we hold then accountable?
No. We want them to be independent.

Can we hold them accountable?
No. Legal sanctions are virtually impossible.

Do we hold them accountable?
No.

To combine the three questions we can say: We shouldn't hold justices accountable, we can't, and we don't.

In addition to this combination, there are five others:

We should hold people accountable, we can, and we do.

We should hold people accountable, we could, but we don't.

We should hold people accountable but we can't, so we don't.

We shouldn't hold people accountable, but we can, and we do.

We shouldn't hold people accountable, but we could.

In the next four chapters, I shall raise further accountability issues, but now we can add legitimacy and trust to the discussion. The first three chapters will examine issues suggested by the first three combinations listed above, and in the fourth I shall investigate issues suggested by the last two.

11

Contracts and Motives

We should hold people accountable, we can, and we do.

The act of signing a contract plus the possibility of legal action if the contract is broken is a powerful source of legitimacy. It is one of the main reasons we should, can, and do hold people accountable for their actions, especially in the workplace. In this chapter, I shall describe how accountability relates to contracts. And since contracts involve sanctions, I want to clear up a possible confusion between two very different meanings of the word sanction.

Contracts

When full accountability exists, we ought to be able to recognize a contract. I shall be talking about different sorts of contracts, so let us start with the most obvious sort, the legal contract. If I have an employment contract with a company, the deal looks something like this: I am accountable to you (the manager or the company) for my actions. In return, you are accountable to me for certain things—pay, security, insurance, opportunity, or whatever. To clarify contracts in terms of units of accountability, we have to list the criteria twice.

98   Accountability

Here is an example involving, once again, our all-purpose specialist.

Who?	Specialist	Manager (Organization)
To?	Manager	Specialist
For?	Agreed job	Pay, security, opportunity
How?	Meetings	Payment, staff development
When?	On demand	Regularly
What if?	Dismissal	Leave/sue

Contracts require two units of accountability, one in which the manager or the company is the *To?* and one in which the specialist is the *To?* In Triangular Mapping terms:

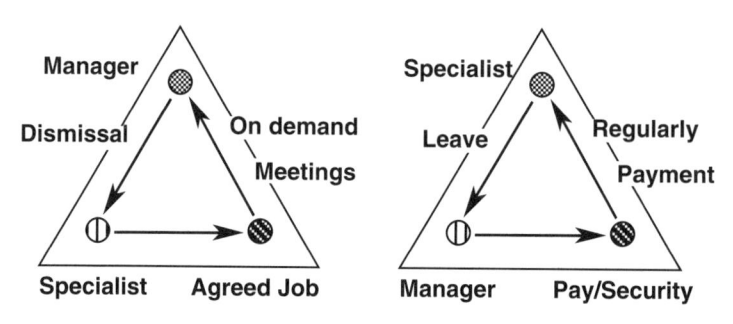

Fig. 11.1: Two Contract Units

We can get a feeling of contractual interdependence by combining these units. The inverted triangle in the combination (Fig. 11.2) is the one in which the manager is the *Who?*

Even though the parties may have unequal power, accountability still exists if the sanctions are credible. The specialist certainly has sanctions—she can leave or sue. But their power will depend on a variety of factors: unemployment figures, the shortage of labor for the specialist's skills, the power of employment law, the strength of trade unions, the individual's attitude to the job, and so on. Since the contract contains two *What if?* criteria, your interpretation of the sanctions will have a considerable bearing on your interpretation of the contract. I shall return to sanctions in a moment.

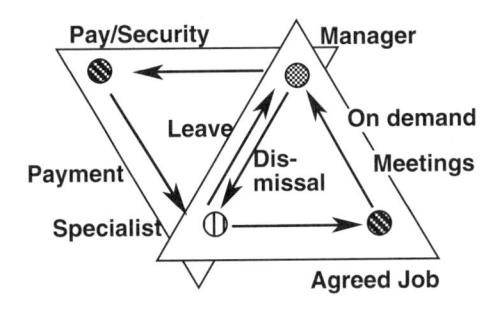

Fig. 11.2: Combined Contract Units

In addition to legal contracts, work in organizations is affected by psychological contracts. Psychological contracts are expectations that people bring to their working relationships whether they are managers or employees. This does not mean a psychological contract could not be written down. It could be but almost never is. There are many more expectations than appear in contracts of employment. For example, you may start a job with these expectations: If I'm given a new task, I'll receive training; Since I'm an adult, I'll be treated as an adult; If I do good work, I'll be acknowledged even if I am not rewarded financially. If you receive no training, are treated in a condescending manner, and your work is ignored, there is no legal redress. If your manager does not understand or care enough about your expectations, then as far as you are concerned, she has broken a reasonable psychological contract. Your ultimate sanction is to make it her problem by finding another job.

Similar to psychological contracts are social contracts. These also involve expectations but are "social" because they include society, or large chunks of it, rather than individuals. For example, it is sometimes said that society has a social contract with its young people which goes: If you work hard and graduate from high school or college, you will get a job. Was it ever true? If it was, has the contract changed?

Or take welfare. Do people on welfare have a social contract with society as a whole? If the answer is No, then presumably society is a trustee. This makes sense because individual recipients usually have to hope for the best, their sanctions not being very strong. The credibility of these sanctions would increase if they were able to act as a coherent group. On the other hand, if recipients do have a social contract, what exactly are they accountable for? Getting a job after a certain amount of time? Trying to get a job? We're back to the accountability values dilemma of success v. attempt.

By now, the fact that competition arises between contracts will come as no surprise. If we include, as we must, psychological and social contracts, the picture gets a little complicated. No wonder the fainthearted talk vaguely about "a problem of accountability." But with patience and application we can untangle the knot of contracts one at a time. Once all the contracts have been separated, we can decide (a) whether accountability exists in both triangles, (b) what sort of contracts are involved (legal, psychological, social), and (c) which contracts take precedence. Here are some examples of clashes of contract:

Linda, a supervisor at Raingo umbrellas, has to stay home to look after her husband who has been in a serious accident. She believes she has a contract to look after him at times like this. (She also loves him!) Fred, Linda's manager, phones to remind her that Raingo umbrellas sell best during the winter and since it is November he "hopes she will be back at work as soon as possible."

The local school board is insisting that a new textbook be introduced into schools in the area. Michael, a school principal, believes the book contains severe inaccuracies and says he is accountable to the parents for using only what he considers first-rate material in his school.

Maria is on the board of a local utility. The city council that appointed her wants to get rid of the director of the utility. Maria thinks the director is doing a good job and feels that a psychological contract exists between her and the director. In return for good work, the director gets her support.

You have probably encountered examples similar to these cases. We are not talking about simple clashes of accountability units here: Whose word processing shall I do first? or Whose order shall I fulfill first? Different sorts of contracts are involved in each case.

Sanctions and Motives

Mention of the two sets of sanctions in the discussion of contracts presents us with a good opportunity to examine the nature of sanctions in more detail and to clear up a common misunderstanding. Where full accountability exists, sanctions play a very precise role

You have probably noticed that, although I have talked a lot about sanctions, I have not once mentioned the word "reward." This omission was deliberate because accountability is not about rewards. There are times when it looks as though it should be but it never is. To understand why, let me repeat an important point: the purpose of sanctions is not to act as a threat to the person who does the job, but as a guarantee to the manager.

Let me give a couple of examples that will clarify the difference between threat and guarantee. If I drive carefully, the police, as a rule, will not interfere with me or pull me over without cause. But if I drive for a year without being pulled over, I can hardly expect to receive a reward for having driven well, say a plaque from the governor of my state. And even if such a reward did exist, I don't think people would start each journey with the thought: Better drive well to get that plaque. As far as driving is concerned, I am held accountable only when my behavior drops below a certain threshold. A few people might be motivated by the threat of being pulled over for bad driving but most are probably concerned about the driving of others. Being pulled over is designed as a guarantee to society—dangerous drivers will be pulled over—not a threat to me as an individual driver. Or suppose I agree to sell you my house. Are you going to view the contract we have signed as a threat? And on the day you take possession of my house, are you going to say I have rewarded you? Unlikely.

We can make the distinction another way: (a) *sanction as part of a deal*, and (b) *sanction as an attempt to motivate*. In practice, there are going to be times when a person does what we expect, gives an account of his actions, and we will be unable to tell whether he did what he did out of fear of sanctions or to fulfill a contract. So why bother to make the distinction at all?

If sanctions are only an attempt to manipulate behavior, then accountability will collapse because you, the manager, will be in a constant state of reworking the contract. The *What if?* criterion will be impossible to pin down. You will be spending your time juggling sticks and carrots to produce particular behavior: "If I tell her this, she may do that. I'll try and involve her, and if that doesn't work, I'll tell her what to do.

I'll offer her two days extra leave, and if that doesn't work, I won't give her a raise." Is this familiar? It may be if you are a parent of young children. Whether it is right and effective in the workplace is another matter.

However much businesses, advertisers and politicians might like it to be otherwise, you cannot manipulate people with a motive the way you manipulate iron filings with a magnet. *You never know how a particular motive is going to affect a particular individual.* A high-powered rifle aimed at his head is not going to impress the would-be martyr. A sanction that you find compelling may leave me totally unmoved and unmotivated. (A slight repetition here, since the word "motive" comes from the Latin word for "to move.")

Giant Motives

But motivation is more than providing a person with a particular motive. To motivate others has come to mean inspire, encourage, or energize them in a very general sense, as in: People around here are not very motivated. This is not the same as trying to manipulate a particular individual with a particular reward or sanction. Real confusion arises if the two are not separated. Here is an example from professional sports.

For the New York Giants football team 1992 was not a good season. Even in the early games, it was clear that the relationship between the players and the head coach, who had been appointed the previous year, was poor. In contrast to the hype and volubility of many other head coaches, he was unusually low key. He seemed to believe that players should motivate themselves. Is this a reasonable expectation?

You could take the view that since players are paid well, that should be motive enough to get them to play well, whatever the head coach's style. On the other hand, football is an activity that is both highly emotional and extremely fragmented. To get players to just the right level of effort at the right moment needs more than money. It needs credible leadership, which may mean traditional inspiration from the coach. The Giants' head coach may indeed have viewed motivation as inspiration but thought it should come from the players themselves. If players expect to be fired up in some way or other, that is going to be a firmly rooted psychological contract even though you could argue they should be professional enough to play well without it. In practice, if the psychological contract is broken, the financial contract may simply not be strong enough to bridge the gap and make the players effective.

What applies to sports professionals applies to every manager. One of the manager's roles is to manage the individual units of accountability. If the people in each unit expect to be encouraged as part of a psychological contract, the manager who by her actions sets a You're-professionals-you-should-motivate-yourselves tone is breaking the contract. So the question becomes: How much motivation (i.e. encouragement) should the *Who?*s reasonably expect?

The Tale of the Disappearing Bonus

To continue the theme of money and its link to contracts, sanctions, and motives, let me introduce you to Doomore Inc. and the *Tale of the Disappearing Bonus*. The story takes place over four years.

Year 1: At the end of the year, as at the end of every year, Doomore Inc. gives every employee a small raise if their work has been satisfactory. This raise is not written into the conditions of work and is, therefore, not part of the legal contract. But for both employees and management it has become a clear psychological contract. It is expected.

Year 2: Doomore decides to introduce a bonus system not as a reward, but as an "acknowledgment" that a person's work is excellent and beyond the call of duty. Suzanne is a recipient of the bonus. It is not part of the psychological contract as it was unexpected. Senior managers hope it will be seen for what it is, an acknowledgment, rather than the basis of a new psychological contract.

Year 3: Suzanne continues to work hard and receives a bonus again. She now sees it as part of a new psychological contract: If I work hard, I'll get a bonus. Her manager, Don, has a different view. He wants Suzanne to see the bonus as a reward to encourage her to work that bit harder and improve on her already excellent results. He does not say exactly what he is expecting and does not discuss the matter with her. Meanwhile, Ellen, Don's manager, still sees the bonus as an acknowledgment of good work.

Year 4: Doomore's profits are down, and no money is available for a bonus—or at least that is what the company says. Everyone, including Suzanne, gets a small raise as in the pre-bonus days. Suzanne's performance remains good.

This is how Suzanne, Ellen, and Frank respond in terms of motives and contracts.

Suzanne: As far as I'm concerned, the company has reneged on its contract with me. You cannot get into the habit of offering people bonuses and then just take them away. It's like a pay cut. I am working more productively than when I first got the bonus in Year 2 and as productively as last year, Year 3. It isn't as though I'm your average employee around here, and they know it. However, I am still a professional and will continue to work to my customary high standard. If things don't change, I'll ask for a pay raise to get me at least to the level I would have been at had the bonus still been in place. Otherwise, I'll have to consider my future very carefully.

106   Accountability

Ellen: Suzanne, and everyone else, must realize that the bonus was only a "bonus" in the first place and it is illogical, though quite understandable, to see it as an entitlement or a new psychological contract. Suzanne will still get a raise, and the original psychological contract will continue to operate. The bonus was only an acknowledgment. I didn't expect it to "motivate" Suzanne in any way.

Don: Suzanne's performance is bound to deteriorate. I believe she was motivated by the bonus and I could get more out of her if she knew the bonus depended on meeting higher standards. I was even thinking of cutting the bonus down a bit as a signal that I think she could do better. Now there is not much I can do.

To illustrate this divergence of opinion, imagine two sorts of playing field, the contract field and the motive field. The contract field has two zones, a "sanction" zone and a "neutral" zone. The motive field has three zones: a "sanction," a "neutral," and a "reward" zone.

Contract Field **Motive Field**

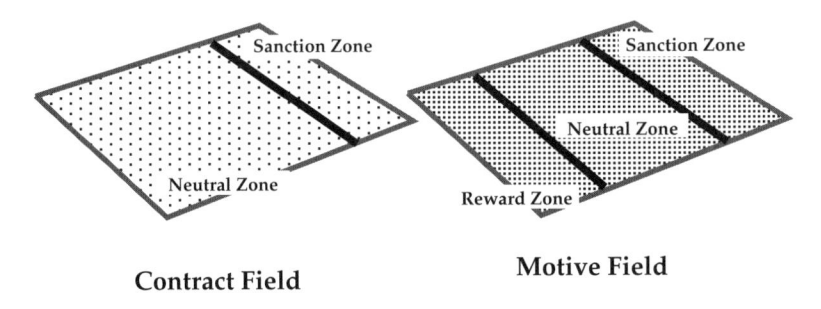

Fig. 11.3: Contract and Motive "Fields"

Your view of accountability will be governed by what field you think you are playing on. The original psychological contract in Year 1 was understood in the same way by Suzanne, Don, and Ellen. They all thought Suzanne was playing on the contract field, and, because her work was very satisfactory, they all placed her in the neutral zone.

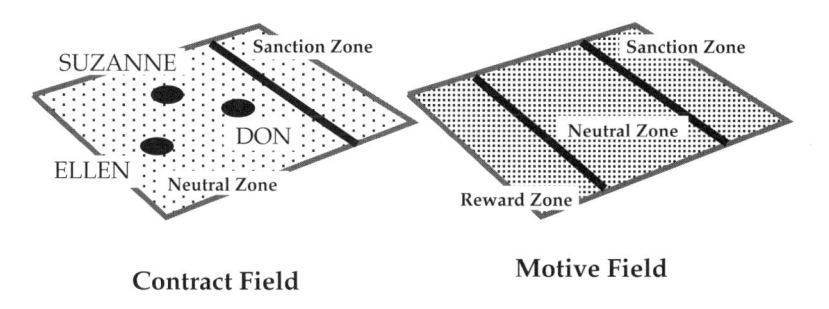

Fig. 11.4: Three Views of Suzanne in Year 1

By Year 4, they have very different perceptions of Suzanne's performance.

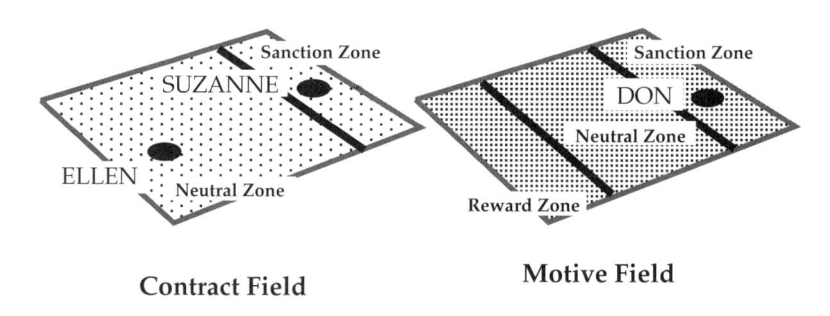

Fig. 11.5: Three Views of Suzanne in Year 4

For Ellen, things have not changed. Suzanne's performance remains satisfactory. She is keeping to her contract, and so her work is on the contract field in the neutral zone. Suzanne, believing the psychological contract to be bonus related, feels the contract has been broken and she has been put in the sanction zone for no good reason. Don, however, wants to play on a different field altogether. Because Suzanne's performance did not improve significantly between years 3 and 4, he was hoping (before the bonus freeze) to use the bonus as a threat to get more out of her in future. So he places her performance in the sanction zone of the motive field.

How could this have been prevented? Ellen might have recognized that the introduction of the bonus would very likely alter the psychological contract involved. It is inadvisable to be wholly logical and cerebral about matters that directly affect people's livelihoods even though we have accustomed ourselves to words like "outplacement" and "downsizing," designed to be empty of all emotional content. Suzanne's comment, "You cannot get into the habit of offering people bonuses and then just take them away," is an echo of the original idealized action/consequences diagram at the beginning of chapter 1. Though her experience must tell her that life doesn't work this way, it remains a very powerful connection for her—and for many of us.

If Don really thought that Suzanne could perform better, he should have negotiated new goals with her and entered into a new contract that was independent of the existence of the bonus. This could have involved a new pay structure, possibilities of promotion, or new areas of work. By default, he let the bonus do the talking, and this moved his perception of her performance from the "contract" field to the "motive" field.

There is also the question of Suzanne's behavior. Should she have taken some initiative and discussed her view of the changing situation with Don and Ellen?

In the case of Doomore, we are talking about money where contract and motive are frequently not distinguished. What applies to money applies to other rewards, be they flexibility of working conditions, freedom to make your own decisions, or doing your favorite work. We must return frequently to the contractual nature of relationships because how individuals will react to supposed motives, "money," "fear of death," "being held accountable," or whatever, will always be hard to predict.

12

Only Human

We should hold people accountable, we could, but we don't.

If the contract is clear and there is no confusion about motives, what stops us holding people accountable when we could and should. The answer, in a nutshell, is Us. In this chapter, I shall show that *we* are often the agents of accountability failure, and that the problem is not necessarily "out there." I shall concentrate on two causes. One I have labeled "The Human Condition," the sum of our personality traits. The other is energy: human energy and accountability energy.

The Human Condition

A common reason we do not hold people accountable when we can and should is that many so-called accountability problems are not accountability problems at all but rather issues of personality and psychology. If managers can't organize their time, that is not an accountability problem, but a time problem. If they cannot delegate, accountability is not at fault.

Here is a situation many readers will recognize. Suppose something is out of kilter in Arthur's division and he concludes that one of his four managers—let's call her Julia—needs to check back with her staff more often and in greater detail, a common accountability complaint. Once this has been pointed out to Julia, it is up to her to do the checking back. To help, Arthur might encourage her to keep a list of decisions that need checking back on or send her on a time management course. Whatever he comes up with, the mechanism cannot force Julia to check back. If she fails to check back, it is no longer an accountability problem but a personality or human problem. Arthur and Julia go through four stages:

Stage 1: Accountability problem. Arthur concludes that Julia seems to have difficulty checking back. She agrees with his analysis. (She may disagree, of course. One of the values of Triangular Mapping is that you can create a map to see whether your version of the accountability terrain is the same as another person's.)

Stage 2: Possible resolution. Arthur discusses possible ways forward with Julia using the units of accountability, the basic triangle, the central server, the manager's three roles, or anything else he needs. He may have to alter some of Julia's units to help her.

Stage 3: Decision. Together he and Julia agree on a course of action.

Stage 4: Action. Julia acts.

Stages 1 - 3 concern the accountability problem. Stage 4, however, is beyond the problem. A decision without action is nothing more than an opinion that one particular course of action is desirable. Why blame accountability, when an aspect of human behavior—one we label "inability to organize" in Julia's case—seems to prevent the decision from being acted upon? Suppose the bulb in your flashlight is growing dim. You know it needs a new battery and buy one. The technical side is fixed. In an emergency you are stumped because you forget to replace the old battery with the new. Are you going to blame the flashlight for your forgetfulness?

There is an interesting sequel to this. When the problem changes from the accountability problem "doesn't check back" to the human problem "unable to check back," a totally new accountability issue arises. Julia is accountable to Arthur for managing efficiently which she is clearly not doing. What sanction is Arthur now going to take against Julia? Is he going to renegotiate the contract? An accountability problem that became a human problem has, in turn, caused a second and different accountability problem!

The problem of checking back can be represented as a triangular map called *unchecked accountability*:

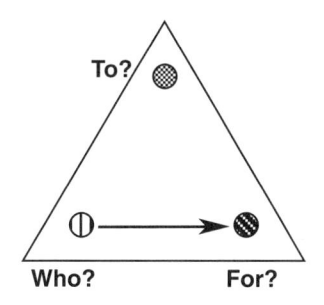

Fig. 12.1: Unchecked Accountability

The action is performed, but there are is no checking back and no possibility of sanctions.

Even behavioral traits we admire may prevent accountability from working properly. For example, merely discussing sanctions causes some people a good deal of grief. After all (they say), it is easy to sound off when sanctions are some abstraction but it is different when you are the person who actually has to impose them. Why this unhappiness? Look no further than common human decency. People who display this trait do not enjoy hurting others, and will do a great deal to avoid having to do so. Therefore, organizations, especially large ones, will never achieve 100% accountability because human decency and compassion will make some managers reluctant to carry out even reasonable sanctions.

Here then are some of the situations in which inaction is mistaken for an accountability problem. I offer a few suggestions.

1. Apparent lack of will

Anton is Mike's manager and also his close buddy. Anton does not have "the will" to raise issues of accountability with Mike because of their friendship. When Mike doesn't always get the job done, Anton hasn't the heart to get him to do it. Here, a balance has to be found between friendship and accountability.

Harder to deal with is the manager who is afraid of not being liked. If managers seek popularity *and* respect, they will earn both by demonstrating that they know how to be accountable for the performance of others. Managers will be more secure if accountability units are clear and tight.

2. Poor communications.

In terms of accountability, the two worst communications problems are not telling people that they are accountable in the first place and not telling them what they are accountable for. Commitment to accountability implies the commitment to communicate. If there is a real communications problem, some coaching in communications may improve matters.

I emphasize "may" because we must not confuse poor communications with genuine disagreement. There is nothing wrong with disagreements. But an increasing belief in the power of communications leads some people to suppose that their ability to persuade is so great that any listener who disagrees with them needs still more communication—or is a fool.

3. *Poor use of time.*

Setting priorities and organizing work does not come easily to everyone. These are habits that must be learned in a detailed and patient way. It cannot be assumed that once the label "manager" is slapped on someone they will automatically use their time better. If the accountability mechanism is not maintained, it will break down. So time spent on handling time problems is no luxury.

"Send them on a time management course" is not the answer for everybody. Surprisingly, there is very little empirical research on the efficacy of time management courses, and what exists suggests that they may improve job satisfaction but not necessarily job performance.

4. *Lack of leadership*

Management alchemy has yet to discover the magic process that turns the lead of ordinary managers into the gold of real leaders. Prudence, therefore, confines me to a couple of observations. One characteristic of good leaders is their ability to make people feel that even the smallest job is important. If you are my manager and want me to go the extra mile, leap over the barricades, take no prisoners, or work with no holds barred, you have to make me believe that what I do is important to you and to the whole organization. I am unlikely to follow you unless you treat me and my job with respect. If you do show me respect, I will follow; and if I follow, you will be a leader. And if people do not follow you, no amount of books, tapes, or courses will make you a leader. Being in charge is just being in charge. To be a leader is to have followers. If you are interested in being a leader ask: Who is following me? If the answer is Nobody, then ask: Who do I follow, and why?

Incidentally, some management writers make a distinction between leaders and managers on the basis of what they do. Leaders are planners and "strategists," managers manage the operation. Accountability knows no such distinction because a job is a job; it is done or it isn't. Accountability is no snob. It does not care what people are accountable for as long as every single unit is clear.

5. *Unable to delegate.*
Many managers find delegating difficult because it seems inseparable from issues of personality. If you are a manager who finds accountability is suffering because you cannot delegate, ask yourself whether any of the following apply. I shall personalize the points by using the name Martin.

1. You demand a level of perfection that the job does not require. *Ask yourself*: How does my quest for perfection hinder Martin from getting things done?

2. You feel Martin does not have the ability or has performed similar jobs poorly in the past. *Ask yourself*: Is he able to learn? Can I train him? Can anyone else train him?

3. You believe the job is too crucial to be delegated to Martin. *Ask yourself*: Is it really too crucial? Am I scared of the consequences of his possible failure?

4. You feel Martin has insufficient initiative. *Ask yourself*: Do I welcome initiative? What would I do if Martin took the initiative and made a mess of things?

5. You find it hard to ask or tell Martin to do things. *Ask yourself*: Am I blocking the accountability flow by not delegating?

Energy: Human and Accountability

Unlike the physical world with its joules and calories, there are no units that measure a manager's energy when we are using energy in the sense of: She gives off a lot of energy, or: He seems to energize the people he works with. Despite the ingenuity of the many people who think about organizations, I have yet to come across the Unit of Management Energy, the UME, I suppose we would call it. Yet energy is important. The absence of energy is a frequent reason things don't get done and accountability is missing. In this section I shall make a distinction between two sorts of energy: energy in the sense I have just described, *human energy*, and *accountability energy*, something altogether different. Let's begin with the accountability energy.

The accountability mechanism, like any mechanism, needs energy. Energy has to be replenished constantly or the mechanism will develop problems. If you look at the accountability energy map on page 117, you will see that the different units represent different types of accountability. For the purposes of explanation, I am assuming each manager manages only one unit.

Unit 1 Accountability in this unit is neutral. Mark has a well-established position in the organization, and reports regularly to Rosalind. But Rosalind is overdependent on him and the idea that she would exercise sanctions is not very credible.

Unit 2 Mark holds Jerry fully accountable. He regularly wants to know what is going on and negotiates Jerry's "contract" very carefully.

Unit 3 Jerry does not check up on Tracy very much and assumes she is getting on with her job. It is not clear whether he is trusting her deliberately or thoughtlessly.

Unit 4 Neutral accountability again. It is unlikely that Tracy will take sanctions against Beverly.

If we compare accountability to heat, we can say that the units are of different temperatures. Different amounts of energy are being put into creating and building full accountability. Unit 2 is hot, units 1 and 4 are warm but unit 3 is cool. (If accountability were at absolute zero it would be cold.) We know what is wrong with units 1, 3, and 4 and what, in general terms, has to be repaired. More accountability energy is needed. Rosalind, Jerry, and Tracy will have to find ways of closing the gaps. When they do, the temperature of the units in which they are the *To?s* will rise.

Human energy is altogether different. The diagram on page 119 echoes the accountability energy diagram in that the same names are in the same position relative to one another, but all traces of accountability have been removed. This diagram depicts the energy people give off as they set about their daily work. (The bigger the circle or ellipse, the more energy is given off. Ellipses indicate that energy is "pulled" in particular directions.) Some people give off a lot of energy. These "firers-up" are the supernovae in an organization. Others are in a state of energy equilibrium, they give off energy but they absorb it as well. Others are energy drains. Like black holes they absorb the energy around them but give off very little.

Rosalind. Energy probably got Rosalind her senior position. Some of it obviously goes in Mark's direction, but it is clear from the elliptical shape that concerns apart from Mark and his department, are attracting it.

Mark. Although the Mark-Jerry unit of accountability is hot, it turns out that Mark does not to have a lot of personal energy. He certainly has enough to get his work done effectively, which is probably how he established himself in the organization.

Chapter 12   117

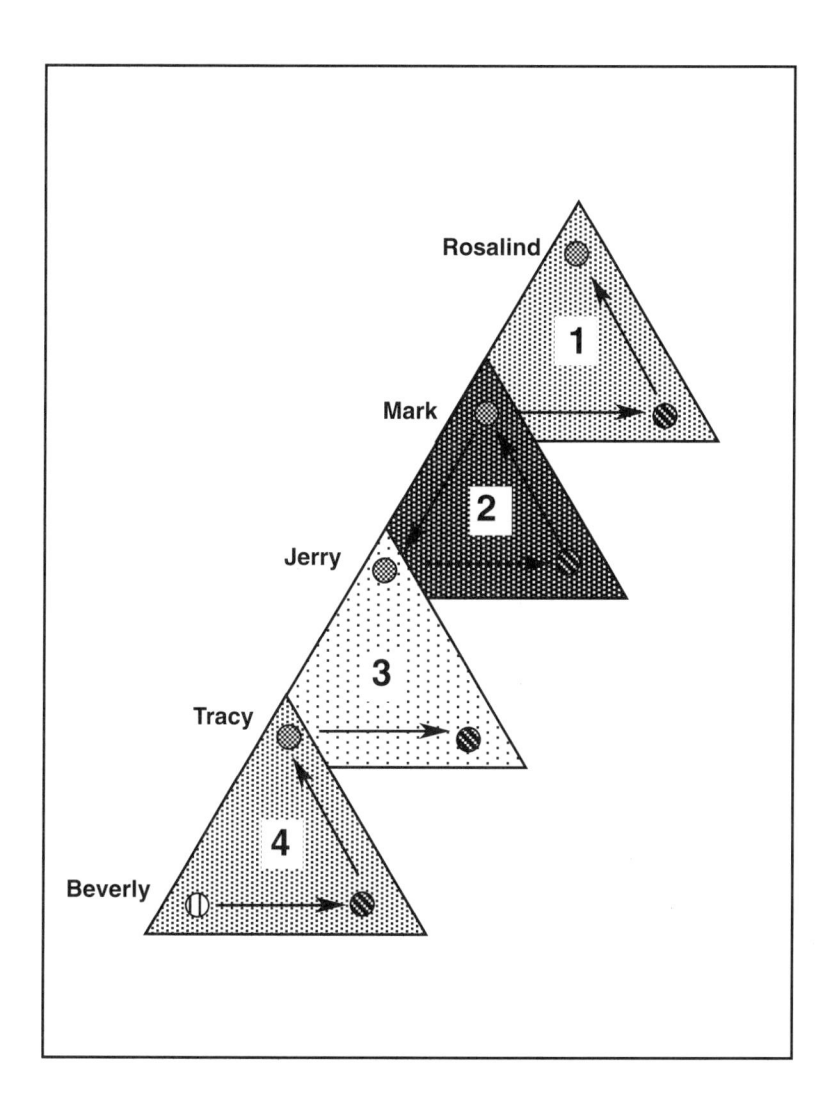

Fig. 12.2: Accountability Energy Map

Jerry. Though his accountability energy is low, Jerry is clearly a vast source of human energy. He has a considerable impact on those around him and he gets things done and is able to push others. He does not check up on Tracy because he assumes she operates like him. If something needs doing quickly, ask Jerry. But we must be careful. Jerry is the sort of person who impresses at an interview. But organizations whose sole diet is people like Jerry soon get indigestion. They need accountability energy too. Management is more than firing people up.

Tracy. Tracy admires Jerry's energy and has quite a lot herself. Only recently promoted to a new position of authority, she is more conscious than Jerry of the need for accountability. Her energy, though, is being sucked in one direction, Beverly's.

Beverly. Beverly is an energy drain. She needs constant supervision. Tracy's inexperience, together with a lack of attention on Jerry's part, makes her relationship with Beverly hard to handle. Energy drains are not necessarily caused by accidents of personality. People who seek attention may not have been given enough resources to do the job in the first place and keep demanding that this be rectified. Or they may be unsure of the boundaries of the job.

You might think that a book extolling accountability would, if given a choice between Mark and Jerry, recommend Mark. Not necessarily. If some of Jerry's energy were harnessed into making accountability work, in this case paying attention to Tracy, he would probably still have enough to fire others up. And Mark should not be smug. He may get caught up in the vagaries of organizational flux; a reformed Jerry may expect more energy from him as part of a new psychological contract; or he may become so obsessed with accountability that

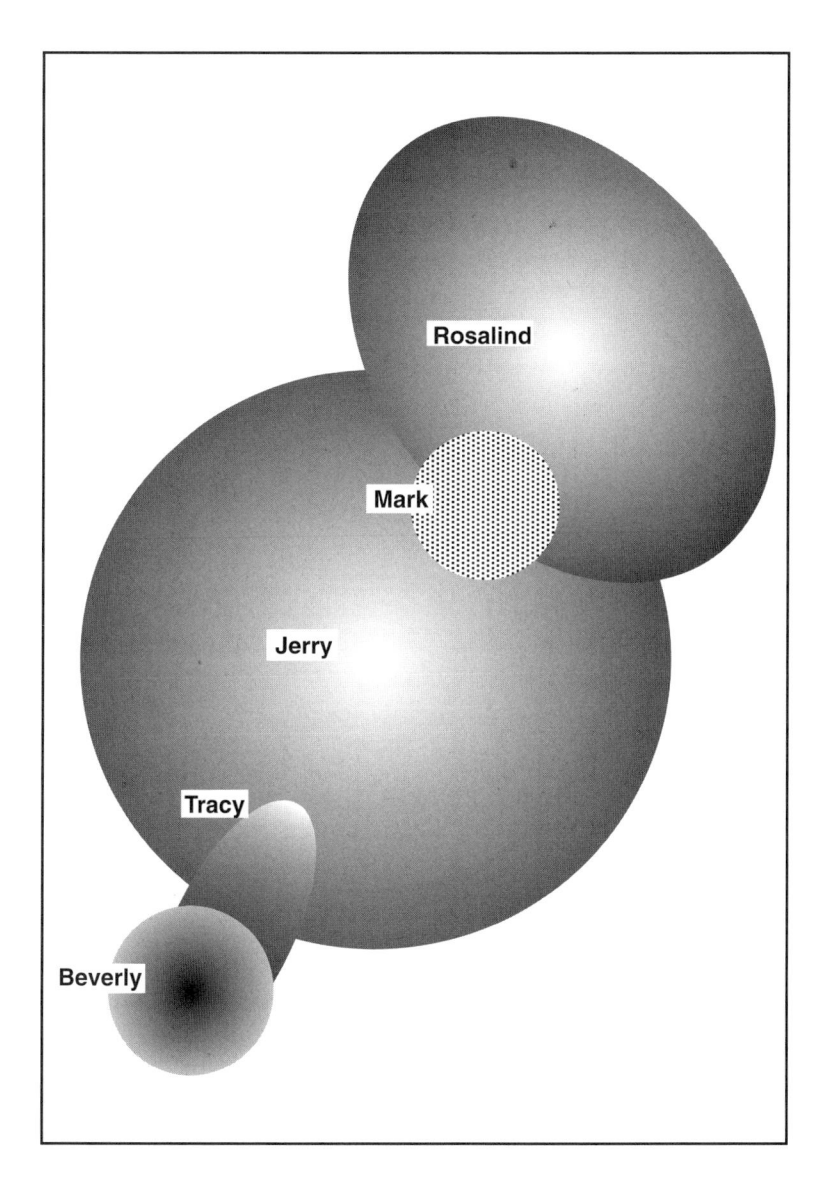

Fig.12.3: Human Energy Map

he loses a sense of balance and the unit he shares with Jerry drifts into overaccountability.

One last point. The laws of physics say that energy cannot flow from a cold body to a hot one, so we should not expect cold triangles to energize other cold triangles, or unenergetic people to fire up others. But we must be a little subtle here. Bombastic energy soon gets wearing, and a quieter, determined energy may be more productive in the long run. We should probably conclude, and I think this is correct, that accountability demands a mixture of both accountability energy *and* human energy. When either is absent, don't put the blame at accountability's door.

This has turned out to be a cautionary chapter. Accountability problems are not always what they seem to be. I began by saying that many so-called accountability problems are not accountability problems at all but rather issues of personality and psychology. Let me conclude by asserting that the converse is also true. Some problems may seem, at first glance, to have nothing to do with accountability, but investigate a little and there may be an accountability problem lurking; a badly defined *For?* perhaps, or a nonexistent *When?* Checking the criteria will be the quickest route to the heart of many problems.

13

Elusive Accountability

We should hold people accountable, but we can't, so we don't.

It is not just an absence of will and energy that prevents us from holding accountable those we should. There are some very real roadblocks. Sometimes we do not have the knowledge and information we need. Sometimes we know what we need but cannot get our hands on it. In this chapter, I shall discuss three groups of people difficult to hold accountable: specialists, senior executives, and politicians.

Holding Specialists Accountable

Versatile managers may command admiration, but not all managers are necessarily expected to know the ins and outs of every single job they manage. All the more reason to pay attention to accountability. Managers have to learn to ask questions that will give them insight into what is going on in the minds of specialists. By specialist, in this context, I mean anyone with special skills, for example, technicians, scientists, computer engineers, and financial analysts. Managers should work with specialists to establish publicly recognizable goals.

One consequence of our rapidly increasing knowledge is that ordinary lay people have lost the belief that they can understand the general thinking involved in scientific and technological projects. Often, to their great cost, they place too great a trust in "experts." Managers when confronted by this problem can try to understand the work of specialists by asking questions like these:

1. What will be the result of what you are doing?

2. How does this fit into this department's/organization's work?

3. How much time does it take?

4. Does the work go along smoothly or are you frequently confronted by new difficulties?

5. What alternative methods have you considered and rejected?

6. What will happen if this work does not get done?

7. What do you understand by success?

These questions need not be confined to the workplace. As members of society, we are all managers when the future of our environment is at stake.

But the issue goes beyond our understanding of what the specialist is doing. A more general question of loyalty may be involved. It has been suggested that technical workers have two sets of loyalties, one to the employers, the other to the speciality. The purpose of the questions I set out above is to ensure that managers can maintain direct and visible accountability. But if the speciality or the discipline gets the upper hand, both the manager and accountability are in trouble. When we ask: Is it possible to be accountable to a speciality? and: What sanctions is a speciality going to impose? we realize immediately that we are back with invisible accountability and its attendant problems. You may be loyal to a speciality but not accountable to it.

Report Accountability

A unit of accountability exists in every company in which the *Who?* are the CEO the board and the *To?* are the owners or the shareholders. Though the law demands an annual report from the company, i.e. the *How?* and *When?* what realistic control does an individual shareholder, especially one with only a few shares, have over the accountability process of a company? Even mutual fund or pension fund managers who invest millions of dollars for small shareholders have a difficult time pinning down what CEOs and boards actually do and holding them accountable in real time periods.

This is one example of a more general pattern, *report accountability*, which is the name I have given to situations where the person or people who are receiving an account or report have no real idea what is going on. Sometimes this results from poor management or a poor understanding of accountability, sometimes from a weak organizational structure. The account may very well be a complete fabrication and, even if it is not, no sanctions are involved. Report accountability has great potential to deceive because it retains the most obvious aspect of accountability—giving an account.

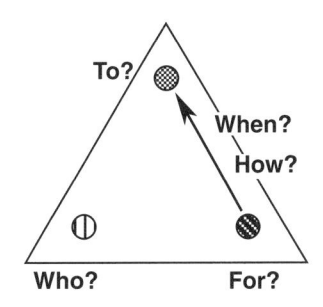

Fig 13.1: Report Accountability

Report accountability goes right to the heart of the meaning of ownership. If I buy 100 shares in a mutual fund and thereby become the owner of a zillionth of IBM, does the word "owner" have any meaning at all in this context? If to own something means to control it, then the answer is No. In fact, I no longer expect to have control. I am more like a gambler taking a chance on a mutual fund bet, perfectly willing to get out if the bet goes wrong. Even if I own the shares directly, rather than as part of a mutual fund, the gambling element still exists and my share, unless I am rich, is going to be very small.

I think we must conclude that it is very hard to create a fully operational unit of accountability at the corporate level. It is a question of attitude. If I am an owner, I can certainly sell what I own. But I am more likely to take interest in "my" company and care about it than if I am a gambler. As a gambler, I shall probably behave as a customer and take my business elsewhere. The more shareholders see themselves as gamblers, the less they see themselves as owners. Who, then, is going to hold the board, the CEO, the managers, and the employees accountable all the way down the chain? If we cannot hold people accountable, we either take our business elsewhere or trust them.

Political Accountability

To write a book about accountability without some comment on the political process would seem to some people a little odd. "Political" and "accountability" seem inseparable, and politics churns out too many accountability issues to be ignored. This backhanded compliment suggests that examining the political arena will give us new insights into accountability.

In the United States, and elsewhere in the democratic world, voters are grumbling. They feel that politicians should be held accountable but aren't. To see why people think this, I could have chosen almost any government institution in the democratic world, but I shall comment here on the United

States House of Representatives which, for shorthand purposes, I shall call Congress.

The short answer to the question: Is Congress accountable? is Yes, and it has been for over two hundred years. At present, 435 members are elected every two years during an election whose rules are clear. If members want to serve more than a two year term, they have to "give an account" to the voters during the election campaign. If the account is satisfactory or the promises of their rivals are less convincing, the voters will return them to power. But accountability must be in doubt or people wouldn't be talking about it so much. So why is Congress simultaneously accountable and perceived not to be? Why should people doubt their ability to hold Congress accountable, when this is, in fact, what they to do? Here are some answers using language with which you will now be quite familiar.

1. *The main unit of accountability is a fiction.*

It is a fiction, though a necessary one for representative democracy, that Congress is accountable to The People. The accountability mechanism allows one elector to cast one vote for one candidate in one district. A voter in Alabama Congressional District 2, say, can hold only one member of Congress *directly* accountable and can do absolutely nothing, in voting terms, about the 434 other members. Even when there is a national mood, for example, an anti-incumbent mood, the power of the individual voter remains limited.

Only by buying into the fiction can one say The People, as a whole, hold Congress, as a whole, accountable. For this to really happen, all voters would have to be able to impose sanctions against all members. Congress is not a board of directors that can be ousted at one go by individual shareholders acting as a group. This state of affairs is not unique to the United States of course. It applies to parliaments and national assemblies all over the world.

2. *Voting is the way members are held directly accountable.*

Let us briefly remind ourselves of the elements of Government 101. The process of voters voting makes Congress legitimate. (a) The act of voting makes the representative a legitimate member of the Congress. (b) The legitimacy of Congress as a whole stems from the legitimacy of the individual members. (c) The legitimacy of Congress, in turn, makes the laws it passes and the taxes it levies legitimate. Laws should be obeyed and taxes paid because voters have the opportunity to cast their votes. Not for nothing was the watchword of the American Revolution, "Taxation without representation is tyranny." Not for nothing have voting rights been the linchpin of many struggles for human rights. Theoretically, voting takes precedence over all other sources of government legitimacy.

3. *Voting is not the only way members are held directly accountable.*

As long as members need finances to wage electoral war, they can be held directly accountable in a different unit of accountability, one that originates from a totally different source of legitimacy—money. Special interest groups can hold members directly accountable too, by putting money their way with the specific psychological contract that those members receiving the money will act in a particular manner. There is nothing intrinsically right or wrong with this, as long as money is accepted as a legitimate part of the political process in the way it is accepted as a legitimate part of daily life. Members have to be wily central servers accountable to voters within one unit of accountability and financial contributors within another.

4. *The electorate's* For? *is poorly defined.*

Special interests are also powerful because their units of accountability are sharper and tighter than the units to which voters belong. They hold members accountable for specifics.

To the electorate, members are accountable for everything—a very unfocused *For?* compared with that of special interests. Incidentally, even if candidates run on a particular manifesto, they cannot say: "We want you, the voters, to judge us only by what we have carried out in this manifesto." Voters have the right to hold members accountable for whatever they want. If they do not like their personal life styles, they can vote against them. If they have just become unemployed, they can vote against them.

5. *If the Number 1 source of Congressional legitimacy is seen as weak, this may have a domino effect.*

If you think the accountability of your representative has been diluted by the precedence accorded to other units of accountability, you may begin to doubt the legitimacy of other sources. "Why should I accept the government and its laws if Congress has been contaminated by other forces?" "Why should I accept a structure whose operation my values tell me is unfair?" Even voting is not immune. A legitimacy nicety would occur if just one voter in a whole district turned out to vote on election day. With this single vote a member would be elected to Congress. Would this be legitimate? Yes, because the act of voting creates legitimacy. Would this *seem* legitimate? I don't think so!

6. *Voters can try and change matters by creating a new legitimacy.*

In order to "relegitimate" the electoral process, voters are contemplating and creating a new form of legitimacy, limiting the number of years a member of Congress can serve—so-called term limits. Societies can define *anything* as legitimate as long as enough people agree. Many states have term limits, and the president of the United States may only serve two terms. But, just because legitimacy underpins accountability, it doesn't tell us whether a particular accountability unit works or not.

Here are two consequences of term limits.

(a) If term limits are accepted as a source of legitimacy, the accountability of members of Congress will still be determined by the act of voting. The number of terms served will only ever be a *secondary source* of legitimacy, in the same way a president's power becomes legitimate through the actions of voters, not by the fact he is legally restricted to two terms in office.

(b) Term limits destroy the accountability of members in their final term. This is easily seen by checking the criteria. In their final term, what will members of Congress be held accountable for? Nothing. They can do what they like (within certain bounds). How will they be held accountable? Certainly not through elections. When will they be held accountable? Never, because they won't be allowed to run again. What potential sanctions will there be? Few. None, if they are smart. Term limits turn members in their final term into trustees. Is this what voters want? Do people think that if members are accountable to neither a diffuse electorate nor special interest groups, they will make wiser decisions?

If voters are dissatisfied with the current state of accountability, rather than ask the question: How do we make Congress more accountable? they should first ask: *"What sort of accountability do we really want?"* This is one of the best questions any *To?* can be asked. And this isn't the only general lesson politics can teach. Look again at the other issues involved: central servers; a vague *For?*; competing sources of legitimacy; and the reminder that legitimate actions may not always promote accountability.

14

Hold the Accountability

We shouldn't hold people accountable, but we could.

When I discussed trust, I said there were many more legitimate actions than we could hold people accountable for. I shall now discuss three issues at the boundary of accountability where there is debate as to whether we should or should not hold people accountable. First, is it right to hold people accountable if the consequences of their actions are unintentional and unforeseeable? Second, what issues should we not hold a person accountable for even when we have the power? Third, can we hold teams accountable?

Intentions

In a violent and melodramatic scene in James Cameron's movie *Terminator 2*, the heroine, Sarah Connor, tries to kill a scientist by shooting up his house. She knows (this is science fiction) that the scientist is about to perfect a computer chip to be incorporated into the defenses of the United States. She also knows that this will result in a nuclear war and a world taken over by machines. Therefore, no scientist: no war. The scientist survives, but in the discussion that follows, he is so persuaded by her evidence, he agrees to join her in blowing up his own factory to stop this chain of events.

This is only an extreme version of one of the hardest accountability questions of all. It is really in two parts: Is it right to hold people responsible for the unintended consequences of their actions? and if the answer is Yes: How do we hold them accountable? These questions are directly related to various accountability values dilemmas: consequences of actions v. just the actions themselves; good results v. good decisions; and successes v. attempts at success. The law has a lot to say about this and many cases revolve round the question of whether an act was intentional. The accused shot the victim but didn't intend to kill him. The accused only meant to rob the old lady. How was he to know she was going to have a heart attack? The accused only wanted to shut the baby up not kill her. The matter is never cut and dried.

Whether we should or shouldn't hold people accountable for the unintended consequences of their actions revolves, in part, around a "handicap" we all have. None of us possess Sarah Connor's foresight. We don't *know* that machines are going to take over the world. We don't know that we are going to destroy the Ozone layer. We don't know that our actions are going to create a world fit for cockroaches rather than humans. (Who is "we" in all this, anyhow?) We don't even know that the sun is going to rise tomorrow, although we would be pretty happy to bet on it. The issue comes down to what we should expect people to foresee. Here are four instances of unexpected consequences for you to consider. Ask yourself how much is foreseeable and how much is preventable.

1. A drugs manufacturer creates a new drug which may benefit sufferers from a disease prevalent in a foreign country. The manufacturer tests out the drug in the country and the results are so encouraging that the drug is rushed there. Suddenly, out of the blue, the drug appears to be causing fatalities that are not confined to any part of the country or any group. Eventually the puzzle is solved when it is realized that the fatalities occur when a local fruit is in season. Mixing the

fruit and the drug can sometimes be lethal. *How far should the relatives of the victims be able to hold the manufacturer accountable for this unforeseen consequence?*

2. A chief financial officer is under pressure to increase his company's revenues. A bank offers him this deal: We will invest $50 million dollars of your company's money and link the investment to interest rates. If interest rates go down, you will actually make a profit. Interest rates are beginning to fall, are you interested? The chief financial officer and senior executives approve the deal, interest rates fall, and the company makes money. Then rates rise and keep on rising. The company cannot get out of the deal and starts to lose money. *Should the company be able to hold the bank accountable for giving them bad advice?*

3. Noreen, vice president of the manufacturing department, plans to fill a managerial vacancy in her section. None of her current supervisors seems to "have the potential" to do the job adequately. A recruitment agency offers her three good candidates, and she chooses Rachel who is articulate, enthusiastic, and has the right background in the industry. Three or four months later, it is clear to Noreen that Rachel's enthusiasm conceals an inability to pay attention to detail and that she might have been better off with one of the other candidates. This opinion is shared by Noreen's boss. *Is Noreen's "account" that she made the decision in good faith acceptable?*

4. One of Ivan's many jobs is to check the filtration system at a bottled water plant. The spring water is relatively "pure" but does contain impurities in minuscule quantities. Although the company does not believe the impurities are in any way harmful, Ivan changes the filter every two weeks. On one of the days he is due to change it, he is called away on a family emergency and it slips his mind to tell anyone

132 Accountability

else to do the job. Ten weeks later, some scientists, looking for pure water for an experiment, use the water from this bottling company. They discover an unusually high concentration of impurities in the water. This is traced back to the unchanged filter. *Should Ivan be on the receiving end of sanctions for failing to change the filter, even though this was clearly unintentional?*

The case of Ivan reminds us that intention is not confined to things we do but to things we fail to do—omission as well as commission. Much of the debate over the *Challenger* accident can be framed in these terms. Should those involved have been held accountable for *not* stopping the launch?

The Roosevelt Choice

The president of the United States is accountable to the American electorate for running the executive branch of the government. In order to find out what the president is doing—to receive an account—voters have to depend on newspapers, television, and radio. Unless the president bypasses the media by sending mail, paper or electronic, to every home in the country, he is, in effect, accountable to the media in the first instance. They choose what to tell the people. News doesn't just happen. It is the sum of deliberate decisions made by editors, reporters, and journalists.

One fact concerning President Franklin Roosevelt was not widely known during his presidency but was known to at least some members of the press. His inability to walk easily was not just a limp or slight lameness but a very severe handicap caused by polio. Members of the press could have held Roosevelt accountable for this by revealing it to the public, but they didn't. Why not? They clearly believed they shouldn't. Just because they had the power, it didn't mean to say they had to exercise it since this information, in their eyes, did not seriously compromise Roosevelt's ability to do his job. This wasn't a decision just made by senior editors. If a new photographer tried to take a picture of Roosevelt in an awkward position, other photographers would prevent him from taking it. Were they right to do so? That Roosevelt is generally considered to be one of America's greatest presidents should not blind us to the possibility that they may have been wrong. For better or for worse, it is almost unimaginable that people in the media today would make a similar decision.

But the "Roosevelt choice"—having the power to hold someone accountable, but choosing not to because you believe it would be wrong—is something that managers face every day. To be able to make this choice wisely is a mark of distinction and integrity. Managers who exercise their power legitimately, but unnecessarily, appear petty, generating a climate of ill will. The danger of overaccountability is always lurking in the background.

Anybody who holds a position of power will have to make the Roosevelt choice. Parents make Roosevelt choices every day. With their moral and physical power, they can hold their children accountable for virtually everything, especially when the children are young. They are squarely backed up by the legitimating force of the family structure. But in order for children to develop and become independent, should they be held accountable for every single deed, or are there times when they should be trusted?

When power is not used wisely, the consequences can be grim. Jill is blamed by her manager Jack for doing something she did not do or for which she had received prior approval. Before he can exercise sanctions, Jill explains the misunderstanding and Jack, rather than admitting his mistake or apologizing, finds something else to hold Jill accountable for!

Jill's position finds a macabre echo in Shakespeare's play, *Julius Caesar*. Julius Caesar, the Roman dictator, has been murdered by a group of conspirators, including one called Cinna. A mob bent on avenging Caesar's death meet a poet with the same name.

Mob:	Your name, sir, truly.
Cinna:	Truly, my name is Cinna.
Mob:	Tear him to pieces; he's a conspirator!
Cinna:	I am Cinna the poet, I am Cinna the poet.
Mob:	Tear him for his bad verses, tear him for his bad verses!

I would guess that every day, in organizations all over the world, people are being "torn for their bad verses."

Teams

The current enthusiasm for teams makes them natural candidates to be put under the accountability microscope. I shall not argue the merits or otherwise of organizing work by teams because how well teams work is independent of accountability in the way that hierarchies are independent of accountability (see chapter 2). Let me first make an obvious point. *Teams do not equal teamwork.* To call a group of people a team does not guarantee they will be a successful team, or that the members will work well together. If we allow for organizational flux, we can predict that team performance will vary. Some teams will succeed, others will fail. Conversely, it is possible for people to work as a team without being officially constituted as one. For example, townspeople passing sandbags along a line to shore up a broken levee are acting as a team as are a pilot and an air traffic controller safely getting a plane from 30,000 feet to the terminal building.

So, bearing in mind we are talking about teams and not team work, here are a few accountability questions for any team.

Legal accountability. When does legal accountability apply to a team? Can a team be held accountable in the way boards of directors or boards of trustees can?

Contracts. We usually sign contracts with organizations, like businesses or the government, not with teams; and, as far as employment is concerned, we sign individually not collectively. Can contracts be signed with a team?

Legitimacy. If we were to sign with a team, what would be the source of the team's legitimacy? If the legitimacy is "structural," is a team a self-standing legitimate structure like a family, a business, or the U.S. Navy? If it isn't, is a team's legitimacy "subcontracted" in the way that the head of a department in a firm can legitimately hold accountable an employee who has signed with the firm and not the department?

Individual worth. In the context of the team, are we going to treat individual performances individually or as part of the collective action of the group, or both? Are we going to hold the whole team accountable for the behavior of individuals? If Yes, how far are we going to go?

Group accountability. If we do decide to hold a team accountable, and believe it is legitimate, we must somehow get people to be accountable to each other in one of two ways: either they have individual contracts with each other (a team of eight people will contain 28 separate contracts between individuals), or individuals are accountable to the group as a whole.

Peer pressure. If individuals are accountable to the group as a whole, what sanctions exist apart from peer pressure? If peer pressure is the sanction of choice, is it legitimate? If it is legitimate, what is the source of its legitimacy? Doesn't peer pressure fail as an *accountability* sanction—it may do wonders as a *threat*—for the same reason guilt does? It is a feeling and cannot be articulated in contractual terms.

Team Leaders. If the team has a leader, is this person merely a manager with another hat, or do other team members have a say in the way accountability operates?

Taken together, these questions make an important point. Jobs and tasks can be done whether the units of accountability are working properly or not. For example, unchecked accountability does not mean that because a job is unchecked it is not happening. It may be going along at a brisk pace. The same applies to report accountability. And the same applies to teams. Teams may do a good job even if accountability question marks hang over them. But the long-term health of an organization depends on the existence of accountability.

15

Summary

If accountability is as important and pervasive as I have indicated, the examples and refinements could go on forever. Much of what I have said is new. In this chapter, I shall summarize my argument as briefly as possible, so it can be taken in at one gulp.

Most of us become conscious of the rudiments of accountability when we are young. In recent years, however, he popularity of the word and the number of meanings associated with it have grown. It has become a buzzword. Some people believe that there is not enough accountability, others that there is too much. Both concerns are valid.

Accountability is best viewed as a mechanism with six components or criteria. Each component must be identified and operational for accountability to exist. They can be identified by asking: *Who* is accountable, *to* whom, *for* what? *How* and *when* does someone report or justify what they have done? *What* happens *if* the report is not satisfactory? Taken together, the answers to these six questions form units of accountability. Units can be represented as triangular maps.

Accountability flows *within* and *between* units. When the flow is interrupted in any way, full accountability ceases to exist. Like people, the units are often in competition with one another.

When we scrutinize the units, they usually turn out to be structurally and ethically more complex than we at first imagine. The combination of this complexity and everyday organizational flux means that accountability will always be slightly imprecise. The accountability mechanism can help us locate the sources of imprecision. The mechanism has other strengths. It reflects organizational ebb and flow better than formal organization charts; it helps us distinguish accountability from responsibility; and it ensures that we do not forget to check whether possible sanctions exist.

Although the criteria remain constant, accountability comes in different types or shapes, for example, direct accountability and official accountability. But whatever it looks like, accountability is as essential to organizations as breathing is to bodies.

The right to hold others accountable stems from the idea that all fully operating units of accountability are "underwritten" or "insured" by at least one source of legitimacy. Without a source of legitimacy, accountability ceases to be accountability and too often becomes uncontrolled power.

There are many sources of legitimacy—traditional values, social processes, laws, et cetera—and, in practice, the sources of legitimacy are mixed up. People's mixes are often in competition with one other. In the way we can sort out the accountability mechanism by identifying the different units of accountability, so in the same way we can sort out legitimacy by identifying the different sources.

There will be times when we either do not want or are unable to hold others accountable. When this happens, we have to trust them. Trusting people appears to make us vulnerable, but we can strengthen our position by making the act of trusting as deliberate as possible. Responsibility, when it means obligation, should not be viewed as an end in itself, but as a practical way to support the accountability mechanism when it most needs it.

Perhaps the best way to bring together accountability, obligation, legitimacy and trust is to describe accountability in terms of contracts: legal, psychological, and social. Contracts require a rational approach to accountability which will help us rescue the word and restore its usefulness.

Part Three

I hope you already have many answers to the question: "How can we repair accountability?" In Part Three, I shall return to this question and suggest you think out, discuss, and act on the points that I list.

These lists serve several functions. They summarize and bring together what I have already discussed; they serve as a way of diagnosing—particularly lists 1 and 4—what is happening in your organization; and they offer a few challenges. Some of the lists you have already seen. Do not check them off with a triumphant "Done!" Keep coming back to them. I do.

List 1: The Six Accountability Criteria

Answers to these questions make up every unit of accountability:

1. Who is giving the account?

2. To whom is the account to be given?

3. For what action or job is the account to be given?

4. How is the account to be given?

5. When is the account to be given?

6. What happens if the account is unsatisfactory?

Who?
To?
For?
How?
When
What if?

144   Accountability

List 2: Accountability Flows

When the flow of accountability is interrupted, units look different.

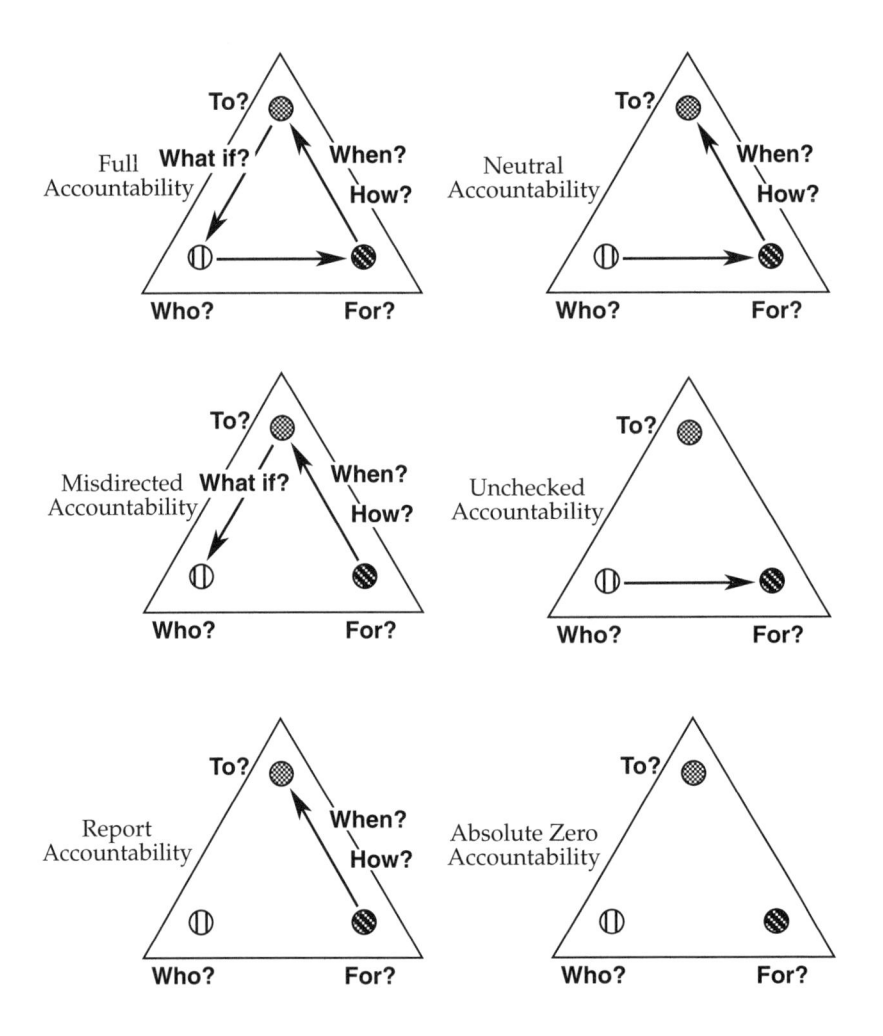

Full Accountability — To? What if? When? How? Who? For?

Neutral Accountability — To? When? How? Who? For?

Misdirected Accountability — To? What if? When? How? Who? For?

Unchecked Accountability — To? Who? For?

Report Accountability — To? When? How? Who? For?

Absolute Zero Accountability — To? Who? For?

List 3: Accountability Pairs

We sharpen our view of accountability by deciding which member of these pairs applies to what we are analyzing:

1. Over   Under

2. Strong   Neutral

3. Direct   Indirect

4. Visible   Invisible

5. Personal   Official

6. Broad   Narrow

List 4: Accountability Diagnostic

Nine questions to ask in any accountability situation:

1. Are we talking about strong or neutral accountability?

2. Are the criteria operational?

3. What central server uncertainties are there?

4. In what context should we interpret the numbers?

5. Do people know what they are *not* accountable for?

6. Are there sufficient resources to do the job?

7. How might our values effect our judgment?

8. Are we confusing accountability and responsibility?

9. Are all three "manager's units" operating?

List 5: Accountability Resources

When you next give people a job to do, check whether they have these resources:

1. Authority

2. Autonomy

3. Time

4. Money

5. Equipment

6. Information

Without these they will be forced to "make bricks without straw."

List 6: Accountability Values Inventory

end results (ends)	or	means to the end (means)
effectiveness	or	efficiency
good results	or	good decisions
successes	or	attempts at success
taking risks	or	playing it safe
quantity	or	quality
doing right	or	avoiding wrong
consequences of actions	or	just the actions themselves

List 7: Accountability Values Questionnaire

To check where you stand on dilemmas relating to accountability values, ask yourself these nine questions:

1. In what circumstance in my work might the ends justify the means if I had to cut corners?

2. Should I be held accountable for my actions carried out in good faith even if the consequences are totally unforeseeable?

3. Since it is possible to get a good result with a poor decision and a poor result with a good decision, should I positively encourage good decisions even if things go wrong or judge everything by results?

4. Are successes all I care about, or am I sometimes going to celebrate attempts and failures?

5. Since it is possible to be effective and inefficient, and efficient and ineffective, under what circumstances do I prefer the one to the other?

6. Can my risk-takers put their hands on their hearts and say this? "I am going to take a risk that is reasonable and can be justified. I know that my action will be supported even if things don't turn out as expected?"

7. When do I expect people to take risks and when do I expect them to play it safe?

8. Since the law seems to dominate everything in our society, do I want people to merely avoid doing wrong legally or to positively risk trying to do right?

9. Although the "quality revolution" of the 1980s says I can have both quality and quantity, which is more important for my work?

List 8: What Are We Paying For?

The For? *in a unit or contract can be complicated. If you are a manager, ask yourself or your colleagues: What are we paying people for? Here are a few suggestions to start you thinking:*

Being on the job between certain hours

The effort they put into the job

What they achieve

Their experience

Giving their opinion

Their ability to make good judgments

Their ability to use their discretion

Taking initiative

Being available

Working any hours

Doing extra when necessary

Fulfilling a contract promptly

Being on call

Being creative

Obeying

Acting professionally

Being able to work in a team

Getting on with others

Supporting their colleagues

Taking broad responsibility

Challenging conventional wisdom

Playing devil's advocate

Being effective

Being efficient

Reporting potential difficulties

Acting responsibly

Being resourceful

Being a self-starter

The quality of their work

The quantity of their work

The quality of the work of others

Their energy

Performing a function

Managing a process

List 9: Accountability Sound Bites

The following sound bites can be used in speeches and discussions:

"Accountability is to organizations what breathing is to bodies."

"Accountability is more than the ability to count."

"More accounts do not necessarily mean more accountability."

"Strengthening one component only improves the accountability mechanism if the other components are operational."

"An organization is the sum of its accountability units."

"To accountability, hierarchy is neither good nor bad."

"Holding people responsible does not improve anything: holding people accountable does."

"Responsibility reaches places accountability cannot reach."

"Many issues presented as accountability problems are not: many issues not presented as accountability problems are."

"Accountability is underwritten by legitimacy."

"Accountability without legitimacy is no longer accountability."

List 10: Legitimacy Sources

Legitimacy has many sources. Among the most important are:

Values
- Religious texts
- Secular traditions
- General values, e.g., freedom, equality, honesty
- "The way it's always been done."

Laws
- Including regulations, codes, constitutions

Structures
- Society's organizations, e.g., businesses, government, voluntary organizations
- Families

Events in a country's history
- e.g. revolutions, wars

Process
- e.g. voting, trial by jury, signing a contract

Money
- spending it as you choose

List 11: *Causes of Uncertainty*

The uncertainty surrounding accountability has many causes. Here are the most important:

1. Competition within criteria
2. Competition within units
3. Competition between units
4. Competition between contracts
5. Competition within sources of legitimacy
6. Competition between sources of legitimacy
7. Organizational flux
8. Computer speed
9. Accountability v. other legitimate actions
10. Unintended results
11. Human traits
12. Human energy

List 12: Variations on Should / Can / Do

We should hold people accountable, we can, and we do.

We should hold people accountable, we could, but we don't.

We should hold people accountable but we can't, so we don't.

We shouldn't hold people accountable, but we can, and we do.

We shouldn't hold people accountable, but we could.

We shouldn't hold people accountable, we can't, and we don't.

In tabular form:

	Obligation *Should*	Ability *Can*	Action *Do*
1.	Yes	Yes	Yes
2.	Yes	Yes	No
3.	Yes	No	No
4.	No	Yes	Yes
5.	No	Yes	No
6.	No	No	No

(The two other possible combinations: "should, can't, do" and "shouldn't, can't, do" are illogical. We don't do things we are unable to do, unless, of course, we feature in news stories with the headline: "They did the impossible!")

List 13: Doing Right

Doing wrong has two opposites: avoiding wrong and "doing right." They are not the same. "Doing right" means that in any doubtful situation you will probably answer Yes to **eight** *of these nine questions:*

Could I say: "This is doing right."?

If it became public, would I be proud of having done it?

Would I be praised for this action in newspapers and on television?

Would my mother approve?

Would my first response to being questioned be: "I did nothing wrong"?

Can I defend this decision rationally?

Would I be happy if everyone did this?

Could I accept the consequences if everyone did this?

Is this ethically right even if there is a risk that it will backfire?

List 14: Unethical Behavior

The explanation of accountability in this book suggests that, given enough time, unethical behavior is inevitable in nearly every organization. These are among the main causes:

Differing interpretations of ethics and accountability values.

Ethical evolution: what is not ethical one year is ethical the next.

Poorly drawn accountability boundaries.

Strains caused by sources of legitimacy competing against one another.

Choices made by central servers between courses of action.

The power of opportunism when people are trustees.

A tone set by managers suggesting unethical behavior will be tolerated.

Unforeseeable and unintended unethical consequences of actions.

A culture of neutral accountability.

This list should help managers predict likely ethical trouble spots.

Notes

Introduction
1 **Webster's**   See *Webster's Ninth New Collegiate Dictionary* p. 192

2 **age of accountability**   *Christian Science Monitor* editorial, November 6, 1973. The phrase was coined by Lewis A. Engman, Chairman of the Federal Trade Commission.

2 **a relatively new word like**   See *Webster's Ninth New Collegiate Dictionary*

2 **a couple of hundred years**   See the *Oxford English Dictionary*, 2nd Edition v. 1 p. 87

Chapter 1
11 **if counting is all**   cf. Kaplan's *Law of the Instrument*: "Give a small boy a hammer and he will find that everything he encounters needs pounding." See Kaplan p. 28

13 **the purpose of sanctions**   For the distinction between motive and guarantee see Hart p. 193.

Chapter 3
31 **style is bound up with content**   See Motowildo and Van Scotter for a related discussion.

32 **Bible story**   Exodus Chapter 5

32 **symmetry between accountability and authority**   William Mayer former Dean of University of Rochester Business School, *Business Week*, June 7, 1993 p. 36

33 **cannot easily be separated**   See Clausewitz p. 104

Chapter 4
43 **The polygraph may create**   See Steinbrook p. 123

Chapter 6
50 **stakeholders**   For more on stakeholders and corporate accountability see Monks and Minow Chapter 3.

50 **If a musician**   cf. Pozen p. 148

Chapter 7
56 **Robert Albanese** See Albanese p. 8
57 **It might create a sense of self-discipline** David Broder in the *Washington Post* Weekly Review, September 9, 1985
57 **Gail Collins** In *Working Woman*, September 1993 p. 109
60 **the company will be in a much stronger position** For a further discussion of this point see Sharp Paine p. 106

Chapter 8
63 **The shuttle program was approved** See McConnell p. 53
68 **They had to prove** See Lewis p. 118
68 **"Can do" but "Can't fail"** Senator John Glenn quoted in Schwartz p. 79
69 **Feynman in an appendix** See Feynman p. 229
70 **an engineer's job** See the articles by Werhane and Herket for further comment on this.
70 **One group of commentators** See Boisjoly et al. p. 218
71 **One commentator** See Vaughan p. 247
72 **built-in tendency** See Schwartz p. 94
73 **only 10¢ a share** See Glynn p. 303
73 **he was told** See Lewis p. 113

Chapter 9
86 **Lord Acton** *Oxford Dictionary of Quotations, 2nd Edition* p. 1
87 **The vice president for example** See Aguiar pp. 4-7

Chapter 10
94 **Here are the sum total of legitimate actions**. There are, of course, many actions that are legitimate but non-accountable because they are not charged with ethical overtones. Would you hold me accountable for putting on my shoes in the morning? A legitimate, but not much of an ethical, action.

Chapter 11

99 **Psychological contracts** The established phrase but not necessarily the best. Oliver Williamson makes a good case for *treaty*. See Williamson. In brief, as I understand him, he argues that the word contract implies a higher arbitrator, and psychological contracts do not have one in the way legal contracts have the legal system.

103 **New York Giants** For a fuller discussion see *New York Times* September 20, 1992 Section 8 p. 1

Chapter 12

113 **time management course** For a brief evaluation of current research see Hoff Macan.

Chapter 13

122 **It has been suggested** Stephen R. Barey of Cornell University quoted in William Kiechel III, "How We Will Work in the Year 2000," *Fortune*, May 17, 1993, p. 46

126 **taxation without representation** attributed to James Otis by the *Oxford Dictionary of Quotations, 2nd Edition* p. 371

127 **term limits** the problem of accountability in the final term is echoed in Axelrod p. 183

Chapter 14

133 **If a new photographer** Doris Cairns Goodwin, a Roosevelt biographer, related this story on *Booknotes*, C-Span cable television network on January 1, 1995.

133 **Cinna the Poet** William Shakespeare, *Julius Caesar*, Act 3, Scene 3.

List 13

157 Notice two different issues raised by the questions (1) Is this a right action? and (2) Does the action produce right consequences? This distinction is at the heart of many ethical controversies. It boils down to this: Are actions *intrinsically* ethical or should they only be judged by the *consequences* they have.

List 14

158 **unethical behavior is inevitable** I am not talking about anything as abstract as sinfulness. I am merely multiplying, so to speak, the amount of time people are trustees, by the number of opportunities they have to do wrong, by the amount of ambiguity related to ethics and values.

Bibliography

This bibliography is restricted to works mentioned in the text or the notes.

Aguilar, Francis J. 1994. *Managing Corporate Ethics: Learning from America's Ethical Companies How to Supercharge Business Performance.* New York: Oxford University Press.

Albanese, Robert. 1978. *Managing toward Accountability for Performance.* Burr Ridge, IL: Irwin.

Axelrod, Robert. 1984. *The Evolution of Cooperation.* New York: Basic Books.

Boisjoly, Russell et al. 1989. "Roger Boisjoly and the *Challenger* Disaster: The Ethical Dimension," *Journal of Business Ethics* v. 8 pp. 217-231.

Clausewitz, Carl von. 1968. *On War.* Edited by Anatol Rapaport, London: Penguin.

Feynman, Richard P. 1988. *What Do You Care What Other People Think?* New York: W.W. Norton.

Glynn, Lenny. 1986. "Coping with Disaster," *Institutional Investor* v. 20 pp. 303-306.

Hart, H.L.A. 1961. *The Concept of Law.* Oxford: Oxford University Press.

Herket, Joseph R. 1991. "Management's Hat Trick: The Misuse of 'Engineering Judgment' in the *Challenger* Incident," *Journal of Business Ethics* v. 10 pp. 617-621.

Hoff Macan, Therese. 1994. "Time Management: Test of a Process Model," *Journal of Applied Psychology* v. 79 No. 3 pp. 381-391.

Kaplan, Abraham. 1964. *The Conduct of Inquiry.* San Francisco: Chandler.

Lewis, Richard S. 1988. *Challenger: The Final Voyage.* New York: Columbia University Press.

McConnell, Malcolm. 1987. *Challenger: A Major Malfunction.* New York: Doubleday.

Monks, Robert and Minow, Nell. 1991. *Power and Accountability.* New York: Harper.

Motowildo, Stephan J. and Van Scotter, James R. 1994. "Evidence That Task Performance Should Be Distinguished from Contextual Performance," *Journal of Applied Psychology* v. 79 No. 4 pp. 475-480.

Pozen, Robert C. 1994. "Institutional Investors: The Reluctant Activists," *Harvard Business Review* January-February pp. 140-149.

Schwartz, Howard 1990. *Narcissistic Process and Corporate Decay.* New York: NYU Press.

Sharp Paine, Lynn. 1994. "Managing for Organizational Integrity," *Harvard Business Review* March-April pp. 106-117.

Steinbrook, Robert. 1992. "The Polygraph Test—A Flawed Diagnostic Method," *The New England Journal of Medicine* v. 327 pp. 122-123.

Vaughan, Diane. 1990. "Autonomy, Interdependence and Social Control: NASA and the Space Shuttle Challenger," *Administrative Science Quarterly* v. 35 pp. 225-257

Werhane, Patricia H. 1991. "Engineers and Management: The Challenge of the *Challenger* Incident," *Journal of Business Ethics* v. 10 pp. 605-617.

Williamson, Oliver. 1990. "The Firm as a Nexus of Treaties: An Introduction," in Aoki M. et al., *The Firm as a Nexus of Treaties.* Newbury Park, CA: Sage.

Index

Acton, Lord   86
absolute zero accountability   20, 144
accountability boundaries   29-30
accountability, definition of   2
accountability mechanism   12, 14, 15-28, 137-138
accountability resources   32-33, 118, 146, 147
accountability sound bites   153
accountability values   33-36, 146, 148, 149-150, 157
accountants   10
actions/consequences   7-8, 11, 71, 108
"Age of Accountability"   2, 159
Aguiar, Francis J.   160
Albanese, Robert   57, 160
American Revolution   80, 126
Apollo program   63, 72
authority   32, 147
AIDS tests   43
autonomy   32, 147
Axelrod, Robert   161

Barey, Stephen R.   161
"Bricks without straw"   32, 147
broad accountability   60-61, 145
Broder, David   160
bypassed supervisor   41-42

Cameron, James   129
Carrington, Lord   57
central server   23-24, 73
chains of accountability   20-21
Challenger Space Shuttle   5, 64-74, 83, 132
Clausewitz, Carl von   159
Collins, Gail   57
Columbia Space Shuttle   74
communications   112
Congress of the United States   12, 44, 71, 124-128
contract   97-101, 135, 138, 155
criteria   16, 18, 22, 29-45, 61, 119, 137, 143, 146, 153
customer service 43, 44

delegation   114

deliberate trust   91-93
direct accountability   49-51, 53, 84-85, 145
drugs test   43

empowerment   36
energy   115-120, 155
Engman, Lewis A.   159
ethics   87, 158, 162

Falkland Islands   57
Feynman, Richard   69
fiduciary duty   92
financial accountability   10
flow of accountability   18, 144
flux   26-28, 155
full accountability   18, 144

genetic tests   43
Glenn, John   160
Goodwin, Doris Cairns   161

Hart, H.L.A.   159
Herket, Joseph R.   160
hierarchies   22-23, 134
Hoff Macan, Therese   161
House of Representatives   124-128

IBM 123
indirect accountability   49-51, 53, 84-85, 145
information   32
intentions   129-132
invisible accountability   51-53, 70, 85-86, 122, 145

Julius Caesar   133-134

Kaplan's *Law of the Instrument*   159
Kiechell, William   161
Kennedy Space Center   65, 66, 73

laws   11
leadership   113-114
legal contract   97-99, 138
legitimacy   77-88, 89, 95, 135, 138, 153, 154, 155
"LoCal" responsibility   57
Lockheed   64

166 Accountability

management by objectives 36
manager's three roles 24-26, 146
Marshall Space Center 66, 69
Mayer, William 159
McAuliffe, Christa 66
Mexico 29
misdirected accountability 40, 144
Mississippi River 77, 79
Monks R. and Minow N. 159
monopolies 50
Morton Thiokol Inc. (MTI) 63-74, 83
Moses 32
motive field 106-107
motivation 2, 101-108
Motowildo S. and Van Scotter J. 159

narrow accountability 60-61, 145
National Air and Space Administration (NASA) 63-74, 83
NATO 57
neutral accountability 9, 19, 20, 29, 115, 116, 144, 145, 146
New York Giants 103-104
Nixon, President Richard 2, 63
nonprofits 50

official accountability 55-57, 145
official responsibility 55-57
organization charts 22, 28
O-Rings 65, 66, 73
Otis, James 161
overaccountability 2, 3, 30, 118, 133, 145

peer pressure 135-136
personal accountability 55-57, 145
personal responsibility 55-57
Pharaoh 32
political accountability 124-128
polygraph tests 43
Pozen, Robert C. 159
psychological contract 99-101, 104, 106-108, 138, 161

report accountability 122-124, 136, 144
representative democracy 125-128
responsibility 45-47, 90-91, 146, 153
Roosevelt, President F. D. 132-133
Rogers Commission 67, 68, 70, 73
sanctions 13, 44, 101-108
Savings and Loan failures 47
Schwartz, Howard 72, 160
Securities and Exchange Commission (SEC) 85

sexual harassment 58-59
Shakespeare, William 133
skills 11
social contract 99-101, 138
sources of legitimacy
   events 80-81
   laws 80
   money 81-82
   process 80, 125-128
   structures 81
   values 80
special interests 126-128
specialists 121-122
split group 40
stakeholders 50, 85
strong accountability 9, 29, 145
style 31, 58
sunk cost 43
support 32
Supreme Court of the United States 92, 94
symbolic accountability 57

teams 134-136
"Tear him for his bad verses" 134
"telephone" party game 23
Terminator 2 129
term limits 127-128
"thoughtless" trust 93
time management 110, 113, 161
tone and direction 58-60, 72
triangular mapping 18, 36, 40, 98
turf war 24
trust 89-95, 138
trustees 91-94

unchecked accountability 101, 136, 144
underaccountability 2, 3, 30, 145
units of accountability 18, 72, 88, 125
Unit of Management Energy 115

Vaughan, Diane 160
visible accountability 53, 145

Webster's 1, 159
Werhane, Patricia H. 160
Wall Street Journal 73
Washington, George 81
"whispers" party game 23
will, lack of 112
Williamson, Oliver 161

Further Information

This book is published in paperback and hardback. For more copies of the book, further information on Akkad Press, or further information on the author, please write to:

Akkad Press
P.O. Box 3076
Clifton, NJ 07012-0376

or phone:

(201) 778-4878

or fax:

(201) 778-4871